SCOTTISH
TRADITIONAL
MUSIC

Nicola Wood

Chambers

Published 1991 by W & R Chambers Ltd,
43–45 Annandale Street, Edinburgh EH7 4AZ

British Library Cataloguing in Publication Data
Wood, Nicola
    Scottish traditional music—(Chambers mini guides)
    1. Folk music. Scotland. History and criticism
    I. Title
    781.629163

    ISBN 0-550-20066-5

Illustrations by John Haxby and Janet MacKay
Cover design by John Marshall

Typeset by Pillans & Wilson, Edinburgh and London
Printed in Singapore by
Singapore National Printers Ltd

Contents

Introduction   1

Singing
   Ballads   6
   Song   14

Clarsach   25

Bagpipes   31

Fiddle   49

Modern Times   65

Bibliography   83

Index   85

Introduction

Folk-music is the product of a musical tradition that has been evolved through the process of oral transmission. The factors that shape the tradition are: (i) continuity which links the present with the past; (ii) variation which springs from the creative impulse of the individual or the group; and (iii) selection by the community, which determines the form or forms in which the music survives.

The terms can be applied to music that has been evolved from rudimentary beginnings by a community uninfluenced by popular and art-music and it can likewise be applied to music which has originated with an individual composer and has subsequently been absorbed into the unwritten living tradition of a community.

This is the much-used definition of folk-music as set down by the International Folk-music Council in 1954 and it is adequate to cover some of what will be discussed in this book. As Ailie Munro points out, however, in her excellent work *The Folk-music Revival in Scotland,* this does not take account of written music or words; or the technological revolution in sound transmission that has taken place since the definition was composed. Some people draw a distinction between traditional and national music, the former roughly conforming to the above definition of folk-music and the latter comprising music written expressly for publication. Others draw fine lines between what constitutes folk-music and what traditional. All this represents a profusion, and possibly confusion, of interpretation. Since, however, all these types of music are in many ways interdependent and are part of what can be described as the indigenous music of Scotland, I have decided to be catholic in my approach to the term 'traditional' and encompass all these ideas in this brief study. Readers should

1

note, however, that space does not allow the inclusion of absolutely everything and that this book should not be treated as anything more than an introduction to a huge subject.

It might be helpful at this stage to try to set down in outline what makes a piece of music recognizably Scottish. Rhythmically, Scottish music is very distinctive, and what makes it thus, for the most part, is the 'Scots snap'. Far from being some kind of ethnic biscuit, this is the term used when, to be technical for a moment, a semiquaver is followed by a dotted quaver. Less technically, if you say a word like 'sitting', with a heavy accent on the first syllable, you have the rhythm of the Scots snap. Robert Burns understood the crucial nature of this to Scottish music and wrote words which would highlight the effect – most people know the song 'Comin' Through the Rye' and this is a good illustration.

There are certain melodic devices, too, which are identifiably Scottish. One is the drone, sounding at the fifth note of the scale and at the octave, which readers will readily identify with the bagpipes. This, however, is not confined to the pipes, as some styles of fiddling also employ this technique. These instruments, therefore, along with the clarsach (the Scottish harp) where the harpist plucks chords at the same time as playing the tune, provide their own accompaniment.

Another recognizable feature of Scottish music is the wide use of what is known as 'gapped scales'. Readers will be familiar with the term 'octave' to describe a run of seven different notes, ending with the first one again. The two main kinds of gapped scales are the 'pentatonic' (five notes, two gaps) and the 'hexatonic' (six notes, one gap). All the notes in these scales can act as the 'key note' (the bottom note), so that the gaps appear in different places in each 'inversion'. The sound of tunes based on the different inversions differs greatly, sounding more 'major' (happy) or 'minor' (sad) accordingly. Examples of tunes based on the pentatonic scale are 'Auld Lang Syne' (and, apparently, the Japanese national anthem);

and on the hexatonic scale, the beautiful 'Ca' the Yowes tae the Nowes'.

Musicologists generally agree that the hexatonic scale developed from the pentatonic, simply by the filling in of one of the gaps. From this followed, not unnaturally, the 'heptatonic' (seven-note) scale. Although there are, theoretically, many possible permutations of seven-note scales and their inversions, Scottish music, along with English and many other countries' music, uses only seven seven-note scales. These seven scales are the same as the seven inversions of the ordinary major scale. An example of a tune based on the first of these scales is 'My Love She's But a Lassie Yet'.

Finally, a word about grace notes. These are found in all kinds of Scottish music and vary hugely, from the single decorative note above or below the main melody note, to the amazingly complex decorations played on the bagpipes and sung by Gaelic church congregations. These runs of notes can be so complicated that it can be difficult to tell where the melody ends and the embellishment begins. This phenomenon is discussed in the relevant chapters of this book.

This, of course, is not the whole story, but only a bare outline of what marks out music as Scottish. For those readers who want to probe more deeply into this, I can do no better than recommend Francis Collinson's book, *The Traditional and National Music of Scotland*.

I would like to set down my thanks to the following people, who provided me with much helpful information: Robin Brock, Pipe Major Gavin Stoddart, John Murphy, Malcolm Maclean and Jane Fraser.

Singing

Written evidence concerning the early history of singing in Scotland is very scarce. What we can be sure of, though, is a truly rich oral inheritance of song, both in the Lowlands and Highlands; though one that varies wildly in quality. Some readers, incidentally, may be surprised to learn that the Lowlands is taken to include areas as far north as Aberdeenshire, part of what is known today as the Grampian region. Most Scots have flinched at one time or another at the sentimentality of some traditional songs, but there is a profusion of beautiful and elegant verse and music, which is known to all too few people.

The tradition of singing in Scotland divides reasonably neatly into songs and ballads, and I shall begin with the latter, if only to demonstrate immediately the problems that arise.

Ballads

Until the task was undertaken by two Americans, Francis James Child (1825–96) and Bertrand Harris Bronson (1902–89) in the late nineteenth and early twentieth centuries, ballad-collecting and pre-serving in Lowland Scotland was done only piecemeal. Words and music were separated from each other, to be for ever parted in many cases. Considering the well-researched and confirmed fact that ballads were always sung, rather than merely spoken, this seems a strange attitude to have taken. The Scottish exception to this van-dalism was Gavin Greig, a nineteenth-century schoolmaster, but more of him later. Most of the transmission, then, was oral, and a profound belief in this tried method of preservation may have been part of the reason for inertia on the written front, coupled with a certain disdain on the part of educated people for what was, after all, most popular among the lowest strata in society. Succeeding generations passed the best-loved pieces on to each other by singing them, and this, of course, continued after printed collections began to be made in the eighteenth century. This was partly because old traditions die hard, but mostly because illiteracy was common among the 'folk', where the tradition flourished, and only the wealthy could afford the few books available.

To begin with, it might be useful to attempt a definition of the word 'ballad'. Turning to the dictionary, we find it is 'a simple, spirited poem usually narrating some popular or patriotic story'. It is almost impossible to be more precise, but ballads do have a readily identifiable style, which is direct and so concise as to be almost unintelli-gible to those who have not acquainted them-selves with the event described. They can be very long indeed with short verses and often a chorus to allow an audience to participate. The story itself is of paramount importance and the performer did, and does, not distract the audience with an emotional rendition.

The example that springs readily to mind, though it has no chorus, is 'Sir Patrick Spens', which supposedly tells of the ill-fated journey of the knight to bring home Margaret, 'Maid of Norway', who was the daughter of Eric of Norway and granddaughter and heir of King Alexander III of Scotland:

> The king sits in Dunfermline toon,
> Drinking the blude-red wine;
> 'Oh where sall I get a gude sailor,
> To sail this ship o' mine?'
>
> Up and spake an eldern knight
> Sat at the king's right knee;
> 'Sir Patrick Spens is the best sailor,
> That ever sail'd the sea.'
>
> The king has written a braid letter,
> And seal'd it wi' his hand,
> And sent it to Sir Patrick Spens,
> Was walking on the strand.
>
> 'To Noroway, to Noroway,
> To Noroway o'er the faem;
> The king's daughter of Noroway;
> Tis thou maun bring her hame.'

The action would seem to place this particular ballad at the end of the thirteenth century, but, of course, a ballad may well commemorate an event which took place long before it was written. The earliest written example is English and thirteenth-century, but this is an early predecessor of the ballad genre which, in fact, made its popular debut about 200 years later.

In Scotland, there was a patchy recording in manuscript form of a few ballads, either words or tunes, but never the two together. The first Scottish printed collection of words and tunes of indigenous ballads was *Orpheus Caledonius,* produced in 1724 by a singer, William Thomson. Even in this collection, only four ballads appear, the rest comprising Scottish lyric songs, in keeping with the current fashion.

Unfortunately, Thomson's good example was not followed by subsequent collectors of ballads and the more famous compilations did not include music. The users of such volumes were expected to know a vast repertoire of tunes and to use the appropriate one, or any that happened to fit the words. It is not hard to imagine the frustration of more recent researchers in this field on discovering this unfortunate practice and, despite their best endeavours, much music has been lost for ever. One man does, however, deserve mention, as his meticulous collecting, albeit only of the words of Scots songs and ballads, formed the basis of subsequent work by Robert Burns and Sir Walter Scott. This was David Herd, an accountant's clerk in Edinburgh, who published *Ancient and Modern Scottish Songs and Heroic Ballads* in 1769 (and further editions).

Robert Burns, who will be discussed in greater detail on page 17, was a champion of equality and was known primarily for his lyrical, satirical and sometimes bawdy verse. He was also, however, a collector of ballads and their music. Unfortunately, at least for ballad enthusiasts, he was far less keen on this aspect of his work than on the song side, but he did write down the words of, and select the tunes for, a number of ballads which were included in *The Scots Musical Museum,* a monumental work comprising six volumes, first published in 1787.

Sir Walter Scott, known best for his novels, also has his place in Lowland balladry. His *Minstrelsy of the Scottish Border* was the greatest collection of its time and he himself was a professed enthusiast of this art and Scottish song in general. It is, therefore, all the more sad to reveal that, once again, no tunes appeared in the collection (until after Scott's death, when a token few were added in later editions). Further, Scott found it expedient to romanticize and 'improve' the text of many of the poems to cater for his public's distaste for the vulgarity of the raw form.

These omissions, however, were not without their contemporary criticism. Margaret Laidlaw, mother of the 'Ettrick Shepherd', James Hogg, prolific writer, poet and observer of Border life, is quoted thus: 'There war never ane o' my sangs prentit till ye prentit them yoursel', and ye hae spoilt them awethegither. They were made for singin' and no for readin'; but ye hae broken the charm noo, and they'll never be sung mair. An' the worst thing of a' they're nouther richt spell'd nor recht setten doon.'

After Scott's work in the nineteenth century, many collections of ballads appeared, mostly without music. The history continued to be one of 'improved' verse and, in some cases, 'adapted' tunes, all suited for performance in polite drawing-rooms.

Happily, the situation improved greatly with the appearance of Francis Child. The fruits of this American's colossal energy and labour are to be found in five volumes published between 1883 and 1898 called *The English and Scottish Popular Ballads*, which is still the definitive work on the subject. Child dug deeply into every source, verbal, manuscript and printed, and managed to restore all the verse to its original form, ridding it, once and for all, of its 'improvements'. So profound was the effect of Child's feat that his numbering of the texts (1–305) is still sufficient to identify any of the ballads without even the mention of his name. After such an introduction, it seems a pity to criticize but although he included fifty tunes as an appendix to his work, he had neither the knowledge nor the time to pursue this aspect. For the accomplishment of this task we owe thanks to another American, Bertrand Bronson. He

9

gathered and annotated the traditional tunes to nearly all Child's ballads, sometimes with dozens of variants of the same tunes from different places. The results were published in four volumes in 1959, and abridged in one volume in 1976.

Although Professor Bronson must take the lion's share of the credit for this work, he himself acknowledges his debt to Gavin Greig, an Aberdeenshire schoolmaster and musician, born in 1856. He became passionately interested in the ballad form and collected, with his colleague, Rev J.B. Duncan, 3050 ballad texts and 3100 ballad tunes, the best of which were published as *Last Leaves of Traditional Ballads and Ballad Airs*.

No account of Scottish ballads, however meagre, would be complete without mention of 'bothy' ballads. These, broadly, were descriptions of farm-life, as experienced by the unmarried men who worked as farm-labourers. This type of ballad has come to be associated particularly with the north-east of Scotland and the ploughmen who worked the arable land there, but there is also a comparable tradition in the Borders among shepherds whose lonely existence was enlivened by company and songs of an evening.

Typically, the account would start at the feeing-market, where these unattached men would gather to hire themselves out to farmers for the next season's work; and would go on to describe every aspect of farm-life and to give warnings about farmers who were particularly difficult and farms where the food was inedible. These ballads have a unique richness of language and humour. The following verses were taken from 'The Jolly Pleugh-boys':

Come all ye jolly pleugh-boys that pleugh the black and green,
It's beware when ye're engagin' dinna fee untae MacBean,

Wi' a fal-lal-lal-lal-lal-la-lal-la-lee.
Reed heidit is the bubbly-jock, but reeder is MacBean,
Neukit thrawn, ill-naitured, losh his marra wis never seen
Wi' a fal-lal-lal-lal-lal-la-lal-la-lee.

He kept five shillin' aff ma fee, the reason I'll lat ye
  ken,
'Twas the breakin' o' a bridle that couldna haud a
  sittin' hen.
Wi' a fal-lal-lal-lal-lal-la-lal-la-lee.

The wife an' dochter are the same, a gaukit pair o'
  gipes,
Wi' faces as expressionless as twa clay drainin' pipes.
Wi' a fal-lal-lal-lal-lal-la-lal-la-lee.

Breakfast, denner and sipper, it's aye brose that we
  get,
Weel we maun fill wer stammicks, we canna tire o'
  meat,
Wi' a fal-lal-lal-lal-lal-la-lal-la-lee.

bubbly-jock – turkey; *neukit* – bad-tempered;
thrawn – obstinate; *marra* – friend; *gaukit* – stupid;
gipe – idiot; *brose* – porridge

It is, on a superficial level, almost impossible to
believe that in a country as small as Scotland there
should be two such different manifestations of
traditional music. On closer examination, however, it becomes easier to understand the reasons
for the gap between Lowland and Highland music.

First of all, Highlanders (and Islanders) spoke,
and to a certain extent still do speak, a different
language. This is known today as Gaelic, and is the
type of Celtic language also spoken in Ireland.

The second main reason for this separate
development was the sheer difficulty of access to
much of the extreme north of Scotland, cut off
from the south by its hostile terrain and therefore
from any sort of influence, musical or otherwise.
There was, admittedly, limited exchange of tunes
by way of cattle-drovers and soldiers, but the
language barrier made any significant marrying of
culture impossible. The continuing remoteness of
these areas, even into the twentieth century
(anyone who has tried to reach some of the
smaller islands will appreciate the force of this),
meant that the inhabitants carried on meeting to
sing their own songs and tell stories to each other

11

long after their southern counterparts found other more passive diversions.

One example, of such a gathering was the *ceilidh,* the Gaelic word meaning 'a visiting'. Of course, ceilidhs still happen and are valuable vehicles for new music, but the meaning of the word has widened over the years. Its traditional manifestation was in the form of a meeting of friends, neighbours and relations, with no reference to class or status, in somebody's house. It would inevitably take place in the evening, after the day's work, and would very often carry on to the small hours. The idea was not to have a concert, as it can mean now, but simply to pass the hours in good company with a bit of story-telling and music thrown in. There were no stars and no separation of audience and performers; everybody got a chance to do something if they wanted, and all in a very relaxed and informal atmosphere. Fortunately, this tradition is still very much alive, but it has to be acknowledged that we occupy today a world of specialists who operate on a competitive basis in every field. The most extreme example of this in the world of Gaelic music is the National Mod, an annual event where groups and individuals compete on a stage in front of a paying audience.

However, such was the grip of oral tradition that some of the very earliest ballads, probably composed in the twelfth century, were still being sung as recently as fifty years ago.

These ancient ballads were originally composed by professional bards, who sang of the great Celtic heroes Cu Chulainn and Fionn, probably accompanied by the clarsach, a kind of harp. Both these Irish figures were supposed to have saved Ireland from various aggressors practically single-handed, in the first and third centuries respectively, but fact is hard to separate from fiction at that distance. The stories of Fionn and his band of followers are known as Ossianic ballads, since their composer was Ossian, son of Fionn, but the versions of these which survived to this century were composed in the twelfth century or later, and were sung to chants thought to have been ecclesiastical in origin. Whatever their origin and vintage, there is no doubt that they are extremely good stories and just the thing for the Highland bard to keep his audience entertained.

The bards, too, have a certain mystique about them. They were employed by clan chiefs and had high status in the chiefs' retinues. Through official clan documents and writings, we know many of their names and thus can attribute authorship to much of their verse. They were expected to undergo an extremely hard training, involving the memorizing of up to 350 poems and stories. The more they could retain, the higher up the bardic tree they rose. It is said that they memorized verse in darkness, with a blanket wrapped round their heads as an aid to concentration.

After this there is a huge gap in Gaelic folk material, with nothing discovered that is datable before the seventeenth century, when we find that the heroes now sung of were no longer figures glamorized by centuries of tradition, but were all too real and fleshly, usually the chiefs and patrons of the bards. These were called 'great songs' (*òrain mhór*) and were suitably laudatory of the chiefs' talents as warrior and sage to keep their composers' jobs safe.

Song

The first printed collections of Lowland Scots songs did not appear until the seventeenth century. Until then, songs passed orally from generation to generation. There are a few manuscripts, such as the Skene manuscript (*circa* 1615), which is thought to be the earliest collection, but these were mostly in private hands and as such were purely personal taste and unavailable to later researchers in the field. Consequently, an enormous amount of material had been lost before any collections were printed and, even then, accuracy was not always the byword of the publishers.

Heading the field was John Playford who published *The English Dancing-Master* in 1650. As its title suggests, this work was produced south of the border and included only a few Scottish tunes, probably gleaned from Scottish court musicians who had moved to London when the crowns of England and Scotland were united in 1603. This catered for a growing demand in London drawing-room society for both Scottish songs and dance-tunes and, indeed, such was the appetite for northern music that distinguished composers, such as Purcell, began to incorporate Scottish themes into their work. John Playford and his son also produced a collection devoted entirely to Scottish tunes. This rejoiced in the title of *A Collection of Original Scotch Tunes (Full of the Highland Humours) for the Violin* and contained mostly dance-tunes, but also a number of airs of which Burns was to make use later, including 'Auld Lang Syne' and 'The Birks of Abergeldie'.

The established pattern was continued by Thomas d'Urfey, songwriter, song-collector and another Englishman, with his eccentrically titled *Pills to Purge Melancholy* (1698). This was a popular work and was reprinted several times, increasing in size on each occasion, but although it included some genuine Scots songs, such as 'Bonnie Dundee', much of the music was put together in what was considered to be an 'ethnic'

14

style. The verse was composed in like manner to give at least part of English society reassuring confirmation that the typical Scotsman was as odd, quaint and uneducated as they had always suspected. This is a label with which Scots have had to contend ever since and one which, incredibly, has often been encouraged and perpetuated by the Scots themselves in the field of entertainment.

The Scots gradually realized that they, too, could take advantage of this steadily growing demand for Scottish art. After a cautiously small publication of verse in 1718, which was well received, the poet Allan Ramsay brought out a much more ambitious compilation entitled *The Tea-Table Miscellany* (1724). It contained the words of popular Scots songs, but no music. This work, however, was hugely successful and ran to eighteen editions eventually, but was far from perfect in its conception. In addition to its neglect of music, which was, after all, just an unfortunate symptom of the times, the traditional poems it contained had been radically altered by Ramsay himself to make them commercially viable as drawing-room entertainment. New verse was added, composed both by Ramsay and 'ingenious young men' of his acquaintance. The result is a work considered average at best.

Despite his spotting of a commercial opportunity Ramsay miscalculated in the omission of music from his *Tea-Table* and this gap was filled the next year by William Thomson, who published a book of fifty songs with their tunes and called it *Orpheus Caledonius*. The melodies, written with a bass harmony, were set down in Italianate, rather operatic, style, and Thomson has been criticized for so doing, but, as Cedric Thorpe Davie points out in his excellent small book *Scotland's Music*, this simply reflects the taste of the day and while it is far from what we would consider folk-song today, it is a window on contemporary thought in Thomson's time. His collection is widely considered to be the first important Scottish publication of popular indigenous words and music.

Those were copyrightless days, of course, and

when Thomson took most of the verse in his *Orpheus* straight from the *Tea-Table*, Ramsay was incensed, especially when his rival's work was a success. He gave vent to his spleen in the preface of his next edition of *Tea-Table* and sought to redress the balance by issuing his own volume of tunes only, entitled *Musick for the Scots Songs in the Tea-Table Miscellany*. The inaccuracy of the engraving in this book is generally blamed for its failure and Thomson progressed unchecked to a second successful edition of *Orpheus*.

The historical context of all this activity is worth noting. Scotland was, in the eighteenth century, a very poor country indeed. She had married her crown to England's in 1603 and in 1707, in order to win desperately needed trading concessions hitherto denied by England, and to help pay the huge debts incurred by the failure of the Darien Scheme, a trading company set up in Panama by the Scots, she relinquished her parliament by the Act of Union. England had gained a partner through whom there was no longer any fear of a French invasion, but the Scots, despite their new commercial advantages, found themselves without a national identity. Part of the enthusiasm, therefore, for indigenous culture, was a desire to preserve, or revive, a feeling of national pride. Of course, as we have seen, the results of this endeavour were not always successful or praiseworthy, but this could help to explain the lack of success of classical or art-music in Scotland. Edinburgh achieved brief fame in the eighteenth century as a centre of excellence for the more formal music disciplines. Continental musicians travelled to Edinburgh to give concerts and the Scots nobility and professional people, who had trained and travelled abroad, felt they were part of the European fashionable musical set. European musicians, however, failed, on the whole, to incorporate Scottish themes into their compositions and Scotland's musical public soon rejected this cultural form as alien and opposed to their desire to promote things Scottish.

The appetite for the native idiom, therefore, was

growing but only a few works of worth can be plucked from a large number of publications. The name of Robert Burns, of course, springs to everybody's lips, but immediately before him came a man upon whose work Burns relied heavily in his own research. This was James Oswald, who with his *Caledonian Pocket Companion* provoked the rage of musicians and publishers alike by including tunes composed by 'Rizzio' (David Rizzio was, of course, the personal musician and secretary of Mary Queen of Scots, murdered by her jealous husband, Lord Darnley). Oswald was, naturally, accused of concocting 'hype' to sell his book, but the story that David Rizzio collected tunes has never successfully been disproved. It has, incidentally, been suggested that 'Rizzio' was a rather convenient pen name for Oswald himself.

Robert Burns (1759–96) was a man of humble rural background who championed the right of every man to a dignified and unoppressed life and who also had a passion for his native Lowland culture. His wide knowledge of music coupled with his unquestioned poetic gifts gave him an unequalled advantage in this field. He was able to advise his publishers on the melodies most fit for some 350 folk-poems either written by himself, adapted from fragmentary pieces or resurrected untouched. His work is written in Lowland Scots and English, but he is better remembered (and esteemed) for verse in his own 'language'.

When Burns met James Johnson, an Edinburgh publisher, Johnson had already started work on a compilation of music from all over Britain. He was, however, not a particularly cultured or well-educated man, and his enthusiasm was clearly not enough for this monumental task. Burns discreetly took over the bulk of the work and with a local organist, Stephen Clarke, who provided harmonies for the tunes, produced a work which was devoted almost exclusively to Scottish songs. *The Scots Musical Museum* eventually totalled six volumes of a hundred songs each and remains a highly important source.

Burns's other major effort to produce a permanent record of Scots verse and music had not quite such happy results. This, however, was not Burns's fault, except in his choice of collaborator. George Thomson was a keen amateur musician who unfortunately allowed his enthusiasm to extend to ignoring much of Burns's advice on choice of melodies and to employing composers such as Beethoven and Haydn to write accompaniments now considered to be inappropriate. He further enraged Burns by changing his verse without consultation, but, while *Select Collection of Original Scottish Airs* does not fulfil all the desirable criteria for such a work, it does include some of Burns's most famous compositions, including 'Scots Wha Hae' and 'Auld Lang Syne' (adapted from an older piece), without which the world would undoubtedly be poorer.

Almost in recognition of the supremacy of Burns, Victorian composers could produce nothing better than largely undistinguished and often rather precious collections of songs, which pandered to the sentimental tastes of the age. This portrayal of Scotland, perpetuated by artists such as Harry Lauder and later performers, has been hard to live with, but perhaps it can finally be shaken off as the public's interest in a return to authenticity is encouraged by the work of groups such as the School of Scottish Studies in Edinburgh. A fuller examination of this can be found in the final chapter.

Is there, for honest poverty,
That hangs his heid, an a' that?
The coward-slave, we pass him by;
We daur be puir for a' that!
For a' that an a' that,
Our toils obscure, an a' that,
The rank is but the guinea stamp,
The man's the gowd for a' that.

What tho' on hamely fare we dine,
Wear hodden grey, an a' that;
Gie fools their silks an' knaves their wine,
A man's a man for a' that;
For a' that, an a' that,
Their tinsel show an' a' that;
The honest man, tho' e'er sae puir,
Is king o' men for a' that.

Robert Burns

Highland bards wrote verse to entertain and flatter their patrons. All this, however, was inaccessible to ordinary folk, who devised their own means to while away time. The Gaelic labour songs (and their close relations) fall into this category. Their musical and also their verbal origins are completely anonymous.

By far the largest group in this section is the 'waulking' songs. These are examples of songs for communal activity, as opposed to solitary, and were sung exclusively by the women who met to 'waulk' or shrink newly woven cloth, in order to make it stronger and more waterproof. As well as relieving the boredom of a monotonous job, these rhythmical chants helped to synchronize the various steps involved in accomplishing this task. Opinion is divided on the question of the vintage of these songs, but there is evidence to suggest that the words may date from the seventeenth century, while the tunes are probably much older.

A group of six to ten women would assemble, by invitation of the lady of the house, and take their seats around the waulking board, often a door, which rested on trestles. The cloth, having been steeped in a special solution (traditionally hot urine), was then paid out by the hostess on to the table, where it was passed around and slapped on

the board in between each person. The accents of the song accompanying these motions coincided with the thumping down of the cloth and the pace of the singing would increase as the cloth became drier and therefore lighter; the whole procedure would take about half an hour, or nine songs, to complete. Although the songs had a story, sung by a soloist, with a nonsense chorus sung by the rest of the party, the important factor was obviously the rhythm and consequently any song with the correct accent patterns was used, not just those that referred specifically to waulking.

Waulking as an integral and necessary part of community life penetrated well into the twentieth century, and although mechanization eventually stopped this, the activity has been revived in some areas, using a dry piece of cloth, simply as an excuse for meeting and singing.

> On women, with vigour!
> Toss the webbing with me,
> We're round it a foursome,
> One more than if three;
> 'Tis eight we are wanting,
> With a captain to steer,
> And if we go onward,
> To the Donjon we'll veer,
> Home of Rory Mac Iain,
> Son of sire I loved dear,
> He may give us the galley
> Then the boat he may lend us,
> She was mended this year.

'You will not get the galley
My hand is not free –
The skiff is much surer
For a crew such as ye,
When the midwinter's over
She'll be sorted with gear.'

What will happen if I ask you
Should I fracture my knee?
And sure 'twill be fractured,
And a sad hap for me;
I can't walk a step then,
If help be not near,
My hovel needs thatching
With its drip o'er my ears.

(Translated from Gaelic, and probably sung with a chorus of 'nonsense' sounds. Taken from *Hebridean Folksongs*, collected by Donald MacCormick.)

Of the songs associated with solitary activities (milking, spinning and churning for example), perhaps the most recognizable and beautiful are the lullabies. The Highland mother had a particularly rich repertoire on which to draw at bedtime, of which one of the most famous is the MacGregor lullaby *'Griogal Chridhe'* (Beloved Gregor), where the wife laments the killing of her husband. To use such words to send their child to sleep seems peculiarly poignant:

On many a wet night or a dry,
And on a day of seven tempests,
Gregor would find me a rock
For shelter from the storm.

Chorus
Ochan, ochan, ochan uiridh.
Ochan uiridh o,
Ochan, ochan, ochan uiridh,
Sleep my little calf.

I went up to the highest chamber
And searched the room below,
But could not find my beloved Gregor
Sitting at the board.

Chorus

21

> While the young women of the town
> Lie sleeping peacefully
> I lie by the edge of thy grave,
> Smiting my two hands.

Chorus

Even lullabies, in economical Highland way, were pressed to other uses, and some of them, it is believed, were sung by men rowing. With a moment's thought, it is easy to appreciate that the rhythms for both swinging oars and rocking a baby are the same.

Gaels have always loved to sing and make music generally, and therefore it is not surprising to discover that there are far too many types of Gaelic song to describe in detail here. We must omit, therefore, discussion of mourning music, fairy songs, comic songs and many other categories, but one or two deserve mention in addition to the labour songs above.

The first of these is the *puirt-a-beul* or mouth music. Research in this area seems to suggest that the tunes used for this were first composed for the pipes or the fiddle and that the form itself did not emerge until the eighteenth century, when the Disarming Act of 1746 banned the playing of pipes as 'instruments of war' and forced their owners, for almost forty years, to use other means to preserve their music. Later on, in the nineteenth century, in the grip of religious fanaticism, people were encouraged to abandon the sinful pleasures of making music and dancing, and burn their pipes and fiddles. This perpetuated the *puirt-a-beul* as a way to prevent the disappearance of favourite pieces of pipe or fiddle music. In time, people began to dance to mouth music in favour of an instrument, but this never, of course, supplanted the generally favoured pipes or fiddle.

The next category could really not be described as traditional in the usual sense, but is a form which has been made to conform to the folk idiom. This is the unison singing of psalms in Gaelic in the west Highlands.

The Scottish psalm tunes written at the time of the Reformation were published in Edinburgh in 1564 with English words. In due course, these tunes filtered up to the Highlands by word of mouth where they were immediately worked upon to give them an appropriately Gaelic feel. This involved decorating each note so elaborately as to render the original tunes almost completely unrecognizable. The process was completed by a 'precentor' intoning each line of the psalm before it was sung by the rest of the congregation, in a chant quite different to the following tune. The results came to be known as the six 'Long Tunes', a peculiarly apt term under the circumstances. Parallels to this can easily be heard in *pio-baireachd*, a complex variety of pipe music discussed in greater detail later, and as with piobaireachd, the form provoked much astonishment, not to say bewilderment, among unaccustomed listeners.

The Long Tunes, as part of ordinary family worship, fell into desuetude at the end of the nineteenth century, perhaps victims of their own impossible complexity, but a similar process was applied to newer tunes and still survives in the Hebrides, where recordings have been made by the School of Scottish Studies.

Much was made earlier of the loss of verse and

particularly music due to lack of any written record, but no mention has yet appeared of any 'saviour' of Gaelic song. This arrived, in somewhat imperfect form, in the shape of Marjory Kennedy Fraser (1857–1930), who struggled around the Hebrides and other islands both writing and recording on clockwork cylinder a huge amount of folk material, supposed to be in danger of extinction, which she then performed all over the world, to the rapturous acclaim of expatriate Scots. It is perhaps unfair to refer to her in this pejorative fashion, but she was born into a romantic and sentimental age, and this shows in piano accompaniments and harmonies now often considered unacceptable; in the forcing of subtle and unique rhythm structures into conventional European classical form; and also in the adaptations of verse written by her collaborator, Kenneth Macleod. It is also now accepted fact that all the material she recorded was, in fact, far from dying out and can still be heard in the Hebrides today in the traditional form.

The mere fact, however, that she did record so much material has proved very useful as a starting point to those studying the field more recently, for example, the School of Scottish Studies, and interesting for purposes of comparison with the originals.

Clarsach

The Scottish harp, or clarsach, is not the large instrument which appears in orchestras, but a much smaller one, peculiar to the Celtic countries.

There is not much doubt that this instrument is the most ancient of the three most commonly associated with Scotland, the other two being, of course, the bagpipes and the fiddle. There are several ninth-century stone carvings to be found: the one considered to be the best, at Dupplin in Perthshire, shows a harper sitting on a chair. And there are many literary references, the earliest of which are by Giraldus Cambrensis (1146–1216), a Welsh monk who says, 'In the opinion of many . . . Scotland . . . even far excels her mistress Ireland, in musical skill.' That considerable skill was needed to play the harp is also recorded and can no doubt be confirmed by modern harpists. Robert Bruce Armstrong in his *Irish and Highland Harps* explains that tuition had to start at ten or twelve years old for proficiency to be gained by adulthood, and that considerable skill had to be acquired to co-ordinate the stopping of a string with one finger while another plucked the next string. There are even places which bear the name, which gives some idea of the harp's one-time importance. The Harper's Pass in Mull has a splendid story attached to it. It is said to be the scene of a harper burning his beloved harp to warm his wife on a cold winter's journey. When he later discovered that she had been unfaithful to him, he cried out (in Gaelic), 'What a fool I was to burn my harp for her!' This saying passed into local common usage, as a sign of despair over ingratitude.

More is known about the history of the harp in

the Highlands, as compared to the Lowlands (but the total is disappointingly small in both cases). The main reason for this was that harpers were part of the normal retinue of a Highland chief, either accompanying the bards in their stories, or fulfilling both functions themselves. Consequently, their names and activities appear in domestic accounts, books and records. This was not the case in the Lowlands, where some of the few indications of any harp-playing tradition at all are references found in the indigenous ballads of the sixteenth and seventeenth centuries. There is also some suggestion that there may have been two different kinds of instrument in use in the two different areas: the clarsach, strung with brass wire, in the Highlands, and the harp, strung with gut, in the Lowlands. Needless to say, there is considerable divergence of opinion about this, from which emerges the possibility that, while there may well have been the two types of harp, they were so alike that they were often confused and the word 'harp' was eventually used to describe both.

There was certainly a great tradition of harp-playing in Scotland, especially in the Highlands, but very little empirical evidence remains to put flesh on the bones of the story. Of the men who played their harps to entertain their lairds, we have only a few names; of their work, we know even less, but there are tantalizing glimpses of what we may be missing. One name only has survived attached to a good musical reputation from those early times: that of Ruairidh Dall Morrison, commonly known as Rory Dall, or Blind Rory. He was born on Lewis about the middle of the seventeenth century and was studying for a career in the Church when he went blind after an attack of smallpox. He was already a keen musician at that stage, so he turned his hobby into his livelihood and went to Ireland to improve his technique. On returning from there in his early twenties, he met and impressed the MacLeod clan chief, Iain Breac, who offered him the post of family harper and bard, a post he occupied until

Iain Breac died in 1693. The next chief, apparently, was not interested in having the services of a harper and Rory Dall returned to Lewis, where he stayed for the rest of his life. Sadly, none of his music has survived the centuries – at least, none that can be confirmed as genuine – but some of his poems remain as testimony to his talents and his reputation as a musician is documented. A number of tunes which had been attributed to him have now been revealed as almost certainly the work of another 'Blind Rory', an Irishman who dates from a little earlier. One of these, probably wrongly attributed, tunes is 'Rory Dall's Port' ('port' means a music lesson), to which Robert Burns later wrote 'Ae Fond Kiss'. Clearly, the inaccessibility of this ancient and remarkable art is somewhat frustrating to those interested, but the lack of evidence is not understood to be a sign that harpers were unenthusiastic about recording their activities, but rather that they had no need to, since everything was learned by ear. To this should be added the fact that a musical career was often adopted by blind people, who would have obvious difficulties setting down music.

Naturally, there is much speculation as to what can have become of all this music. The fact that it was not written down surely cannot have led to its complete disappearance – this has not happened, after all, to any of the other great oral traditions of Scotland. Some, probably many, tunes will have disappeared without trace, but an entire repertoire seems unlikely. Francis Collinson suggests, quite reasonably, that what probably happened was that, after the harp fell out of favour, the tunes were poached and adapted for use by other instruments, mainly the fiddle and bagpipes. In fact some pieces of music, which purport to be examples of ancient harp music but adapted for piano, bear a certain resemblance to piobaireachd (so-called 'classical' bagpipe music). This obviously opens up the possibility that other piobaireachd music was adapted in the same way, and might account for the fact, in his observation at least, that piobaireachd seems to have sprung into being in an extremely developed form.

Whatever the truth of the matter, what is certain is that harpers went out of fashion, and were supplanted as clan court musicians by bagpipers, whose strident tones could be more easily heard by large gatherings.

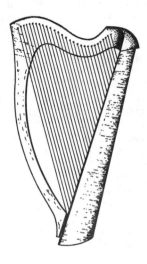

Another certainty, in a sea of uncertainties, is the shape of the instrument itself, since there are two Scottish harps which have survived from the fifteenth and sixteenth centuries, both of which are very similar to Irish harps of the same period. These, however, are the only two known examples. The earlier of the two is known as the Lamont Harp and is said to date from about 1464. It passed from the hands of the Lamont family when the harpist married and took the harp to her new home with the Ludes. It was made of wood, and was decorated with precious stones; it was also much loved and used, it seems, since, as Armstrong points out in *The Irish and Highland Harps*, it was 'considerably worn by the friction of hands and wrist'; he also quotes an older source which talks of specially made protection in the form of 'ane cais . . . coverit with leddir'. All this attention could not protect it from bad workmanship, though: it suffered a bad crack and subsequent warping, due to over-tightening of the strings.

The second harp also found its way to the Ludes, purportedly gifted by Mary Queen of Scots, approximately one hundred years later. Tradition has it that there were golden decorations on it showing the royal arms of Scotland and representations of Queen Mary, but that these were stolen in the eighteenth century. What do remain are many Christian symbols, leading to speculation that the harp may have been made for an important cleric. Armstrong observes that the harp was used to accompany mass in Ireland and may well have been used in the same way in the Western Isles. Both these instruments display a distinctive curvature, which has been dubbed the 'Highland hump'. These treasures are now on display at the Royal Museum of Scotland in Edinburgh.

Happily, the story of the clarsach does not end on this sad note, because, after a dormant period, it re-emerged at the end of the nineteenth century. Lord Archibald Campbell was the first person who made any real attempt to re-establish the harp. He had several made, modelled on the Queen Mary Harp, and others according to a contemporary description. These beautifully made harps often caused a flutter in antiquarian circles, as hopes were raised of another authentic 'find'. Despite his enthusiasm, however, and the inclusion of the harp as a competitive instrument at the first Gaelic Mods at the turn of the century, interest waned after a few years and might have disappeared altogether had it not been for the interest of the Kennedy Fraser family. Marjory Kennedy Fraser was partly responsible for an upsurge of interest in Gaelic songs and travelled widely giving concerts. Her daughter, Patuffa, joined her on these trips, accompanying her on the harp with her own arrangements. Later, Patuffa sang and played on her own, covering as vast a mileage as she had with her mother.

There is little doubt that the Kennedy Frasers gave the harp a vital boost at a critical stage, and enthusiasm continued to grow during the twenties, leading to the formation of the Clarsach Society in 1931, at the close of the National Mod in Dingwall. The Society has maintained its close links with the An Comunn Gaidhealach ('The Gaelic Speakers' Association', formed in the late nineteenth century to promote Gaelic song and literature), and one of its two vice-presidents is always the current president of the Mod. Its aim, of course, was and is further to promote the interests of the harp both in this country and abroad: arranging courses and concerts, hiring out harps, making recommendations to the Mod, encouraging the composition of music, and now, running the recently established Edinburgh Harp Festival, which takes place in the spring each year. The Society has six thriving branches, which cover London, the West Country and Northumbria as well as the whole of Scotland, and has contacts with harp-makers in all these places, as well as one or two in Canada. With such strong foundations, it is hoped that the fortunes of the harp will continue to grow.

Bagpipes

The origin of the Scottish bagpipe is one of those topics which is discussed and argued over endlessly by academics, who rest safe in the knowledge, at least for the moment, that no one can really be sure about it. What is clear, however, is that 'pipe-type' instruments have been in use in one form or another all over the world for many hundreds of years and may even have been played in Babylon at the time of Nebuchadnezzar. Today, variations of this instrument are played in France, Italy, Russia, India and Czechoslovakia, to name but a few.

The most popular theory concerning their route to Scotland, at that stage without the bag, is that they came via the Romans, who started their 360-year occupation of Britain in AD 43. Despite the well-documented hostilities, there were quite long periods when no fighting went on, and during those times the Romans lived quite peaceably with their neighbours, and trade, marriages and so on were common between them and the indigenous peoples.

It seems reasonable to suggest, therefore, that during these quiet times, pipe music would be heard by visitors to Roman-occupied towns and villages and that some may have been curious enough to find out how to make and play them. They were an obligatory part of any Roman religious ceremony and were also played simply for pleasure, though they were never an official military instrument, as they became for Scotland much later. For martial purposes, the Romans preferred the more brazen sound of the trumpet (*tuba*) and the horn (*cornu buccina*). The pipes, in those days, would have had a gentler tone than that of the modern bagpipes.

The extraordinary fact is, though, that there is no evidence that the Celts showed any interest in assimilating the pipes into their culture whatsoever. In view of a long history of musicianship, this seems very odd.

So, what could the reasons be for this apparent apathy? The most likely is that the Celts were using another form of pipes, and simply did not need any more, so we return to our original question regarding the origins of the pipes in Scotland.

Of course, it is possible that the Celts had independently invented the pipes, but it is more likely that they were brought to Scotland. The Roman pipes took the form of two divergent instruments, but in Egypt they played double-pipes, which were bound together; they also developed the drone, by stopping up all the holes bar one, on one of the pipes. This, of course, has immediate parallels with the Scottish pipes; it also seems a more plausible solution to the problem.

When, and how, could Egyptian pipes have arrived in Scotland? In his definitive work on the bagpipes, Francis Collinson makes several suggestions:

1 Via immigrants from the Mediterranean who are said to have reached Scotland by sea *circa* 2000–3000 BC.
2 Via the same peoples who had first settled in Ireland.
3 Via Bronze Age immigrants who came by land from the European continent, reaching Scotland after first settling in England and Ireland.
4 Via the foreign soldiers employed by the Roman army, who came from all over Europe and North Africa.

Although the last of these seems the most likely proposition, it is impossible to be sure, and it remains reasonably likely that this type of pipe had been in use in Scotland long before the Romans arrived.

Alongside all this, there is the fact that the Emperor Nero (AD 37–68) played the bagpipes as well as the fiddle. This does not in fact negate all the above speculation, as we shall see. It appears, then, that Nero, despite all his less endearing qualities, was a considerable musician and loved the bagpipes, which was a popular instrument in Rome during the second half of the first century AD, even playing them in competition. The kind of bagpipe played then probably had two chanters (as opposed to the one which is found today in Scotland) and are still played in Italy today under the title of *zampogna*.

It seems that these pipes may have been rather reviled by purists who played on the more sophisticated 'bagless' pipes discussed earlier. At any rate the bagpipes were never mentioned again by any writer of the classical Roman period and there is no solid evidence to suggest that they were ever played in Britain at this stage. The discovery of a small carving at one of the stations of Hadrian's Wall, which appeared to show a contemporary bagpiper, has had some doubt cast on its authenticity, and it is now thought to be of much later vintage.

To return to the mouth-blown pipes, then, there is certainly plenty of pictorial evidence, especially in England, that they were commonly used by minstrels, possibly up to the tenth century. However, there is some doubt about whether they were continuously in use from Roman times, since they may have fallen into desuetude and been reintroduced at a later time.

Scholars, at this stage, have to 'take a view' about when the bag was first added to the mouth-blown pipes, since this is probably what happened. The first clear literary reference to the bag or 'chorus', however, is in the twelfth century and by the thirteenth century carvings of animals playing the bagpipes were appearing, including one of a pig in Melrose Abbey in the Scottish Borders, though this may have been added as late as the fifteenth century. Certainly, by the fourteenth century, the bagpipe, with its one drone and chanter, would have been in fairly common use among minstrels; and it is said that they were played at the Battle of Bannockburn in 1314, when King Robert the Bruce of Scotland trounced the army of Edward II of England. The use of the word 'ministrel' in written records of the time, instead of a more specific term, is one of the factors which makes it difficult to pinpoint exactly when bagpipers began to be seen more commonly.

The first king who is recorded as having taken an interest in playing the bagpipes was James I of Scotland (1394–1437) and after him, Henry VIII himself (1491–1547), who apparently had five sets of bagpipes in his vast collection of instruments. It is not entirely clear if Henry ever played them himself, but such an able and interested musician would surely at least try out all the instruments he owned.

By this stage, the bagpipe had skipped the confines of court and was making its presence felt to the general public as well. Especially in the Border areas of Scotland, musicians were employed by each town of any size to mark the official beginning and end of each day. At 4 a.m. and 8 p.m. a piper and a drummer, dressed in often quite lurid livery, would pace the streets announcing the hour. The English had much the same kind of tradition, with a band of 'waits', playing various woodwind instruments. David Johnson points out in his *Music and Society in Lowland Scotland in the 18th Century* that the inevitable repetition of tunes must have been as maddening as radio jingles today.

At any rate, these musicians had enough status to allow them a free house and often a piece of land as well, and the positions were usually hereditary. As well as their time-keeping duties, they were also required to play at fairs, weddings, and all other festivities. Among the most famous of all the town pipers were the Hastie family, who were official pipers for the town of Jedburgh continuously from the early sixteenth century until the end of the eighteenth century. It is said that the first of these, John Hastie, piped the Border men into battle at Flodden in 1513, and the very pipes he had used on that occasion were handed down to each successive town piper.

Not everybody approved of the bagpipes, though. The Reformed Church in Scotland, with John Knox at its head, preached sternly against such frivolous activities, especially when they took place on a Sunday, and their use was eventually banned at weddings, too. In the seventeenth century, clerics were even driven to claiming that the bagpipe was the instrument of the Devil and that playing or listening to it was therefore blasphemous. Robert Burns put this notion to amusing use in 'Tam o' Shanter':

> Inspiring bold John Barleycorn!
> What dangers thou canst make us scorn!
> Wi' tippenny we fear nae evil;
> Wi' usquebae, we'll face the devil!
>
> As Tammie glowr'd amaz'd and curious,
> The mirth and fun grew fast and furious!
>
> Ev'n Satan glowr'd, and fidg'd fu' fain,
> An' hotch'd an' blew wi' might an' main,
> Till first ae caper, syne anither,
> Tam tint his reason a'thegither,
> An' roars out, 'Weel done, Cutty-Sark!'
>
> Ah, Tam! ah, Tam! Thou'll get thy fairin'!
> In hell they'll roast thee like a herrin'!

tippenny – cheap beer; *usquebae* – whisky; *fidge fu' fain* – to be restless; *tint* – to lose; *fairin'* – just deserts

Perhaps a word or two should be said about different types of bagpipes. Nobody can have escaped the familiar and ubiquitous sight of a pipe-band marching down the main street of practically every major city in the world. We can, therefore, readily conjure up a picture of what the bagpipes look like. That, however, is not the whole story.

Most of what has been discussed here concerns the forerunners of the modern Highland bagpipe, but the Border 'town pipers', for example, played their own version of these extraordinary instruments. The main difference in these was that the

35

bag was blown by bellows worked by the right arm through a pipe connecting the two, and the sound they made was altogether more gentle and soothing than what we are used to hearing now. There were two kinds of these bellows-blown pipes used in the Scottish Borders: the Borders pipe itself, often called 'cauld-wind pipes' and a smaller version, imaginatively dubbed the small pipes. They were very popular in the eighteenth and early nineteenth century, but appear to have been submerged thereafter by their harsher-sounding cousin. It has been mentioned that they were played at all kinds of festivities and the music, of which quite a lot survives, was essentially, therefore, light dance-music. There is some authority to suggest, however, that a whole repertoire of more serious music existed which has since vanished completely.

Versions of these bellows-blown pipes were also found in Northumberland and Ireland, and it is therefore thought that they may have the same origin – that is, that they may have come from France and been developed separately from the mouth-blown ones, in the areas mentioned.

It is the Northumbrian 'model' that best survived of all these and the sweet tones of this instrument can be heard readily today, especially on its home ground. Happily, the Scottish Borders pipes' (large and small) fortunes seem to be reviving now and they are being made and played in increasing numbers.

To return, then, to the rather speculative story of the Highland bagpipe, the jump has to be made to the time where it 'made its name'. Again, scholars can do little more than guess at how and when the bagpipe first made its appearance in the north. It is not unlikely, however, that some enterprising musician engaged in the service of a chief making political and social forays to the southern parts of Scotland would show an interest in what his fellow minstrels were playing and take an example back home.

It has been mentioned that there is a tradition that the pipes were taken into battle at Bannockburn in 1314 by pipers to the Menzies clan, but this is impossible to confirm. There is, however, written record of the pipes beginning to be favoured over the harp, the traditional pre-battle instrument, by the early fifteenth century. The evidence includes some verse written by a harpist who was clearly not keen that a piper should usurp his jealously held position.

It is not really surprising that the pipes became so much associated with battle. All Scots have watched films made far from Scotland which include scenes of pipers trying to encourage their comrades to fight by playing stirring tunes. This, then, became a major role of the piper – to excite an army into the appropriate mood before and during battle. There is plenty of evidence to support this including an interesting reference in a poem entitled 'The Triumph of the Lord, after the manner of Men' by Alexander Hume, supposedly about the defeat of the Spanish Armada, which mentions 'Hieland, Scottes and Hybernicke' pipes, i.e. Highland, Lowland and Irish pipes; all three types were obviously familiar to him, and presumably his readers, in 1598.

By this time, i.e. the sixteenth century, a second drone had been added to the bagpipe, and the sound it made, therefore, was altogether fuller and louder than before. One of the accepted disadvantages of sound production is inflexibility. Pipes always sound loud and cannot be played softly. This is, of course, an advantage when they must be heard by crowds of people in an outdoor setting, many of whom are standing well away from the centre of activity, as is very often the case. Anybody who has listened to a performance indoors, however, can testify to the unacceptable level of decibels.

The loud sound of the pipes can certainly be considered a disadvantage, but it may even be that, had it not been for this characteristic, the repertoire might have been completely different. In order to counteract this and the inexorable and continuous sound of the drones, music of a very complex and highly decorated nature was composed, which leads us to the next and crucial stage of the story.

Even people who know almost nothing about the bagpipes have heard of the MacCrimmons, hereditary pipers to the clan MacLeod. As we shall see, they succeeded in boosting the status of the bagpipe from a 'pop' instrument to a serious one with its own 'classical' repertoire.

As with all good stories, the MacCrimmons' one is shrouded in mystery. No one is certain whence they sprang, but lore, naturally, abounds and has their origins in Ireland, Scotland and Italy. The Italian stories are definitely the best: one says that a MacLeod brought a piper with him from Italy, on his way back from the crusades. The piper had lived in Cremona, hence the name MacCrimmon.

The one that the MacCrimmons themselves are said to have believed, though, has the son of a priest of Cremona emigrating to Northern Ireland in 1510, marrying into a piping family, changing his name and ultimately settling in Scotland.

Whatever the truth of their origins, there is no doubt about their later history. They were considered very well educated and sophisticated and some of them were quite wealthy, employing managers to work their many farms. The first of the MacCrimmons about whom we can be sure is Donald Mor (1570–1640). He was a known composer of bagpipe music, and is said to have invented piobaireachd, which simply means pipe-playing, the 'classical' form of bagpipe music.

Before piobaireachd (also known as *pibroch* and, most correctly, *ceol mor* (big music)) was devised, the repertoire was largely confined to tunes of songs or dance-music (*ceol beag* (small music)). Although this repertoire continued to be popular after the advent of ceol mor (and remains so to this day), those who learned to play piobaireachd considered ceol beag as worthless and made themselves into a rather snobbish elite.

It would be impossible to explain this extra-ordinary art form in detail here, but basically it divides into three rough categories: the salute, the lament and the gathering. The theme, called the *urlar*, is played first followed by variations each more complicated than the one before: the *siubhal*, the *taorluath*, the *crunluath*; finally the *urlar* is played again. This is an explanation of the order of events nowadays, but there is authority to suggest that at one time the *urlar* was played in between each of the variations. All this would have made for an extremely long performance time, which perhaps explains its limited appeal. Some of these pieces have had words attached to one or more of their movements and are known as piobaireachd songs. Among the most well known of these is *'Cha till MacCruimean'* (No more, MacCrimmon), composed by Donald Ban Mac-Crimmon, supposedly after a vision of his death. He was, in fact, the only man killed at the Rout of Moy in the '45 Rebellion, not long after:

> O'er Coolin's face the night is creeping,
> The banshee's wail is round us sweeping:
> Blue eyes in Duin are dim with weeping,
> Since thou art gone and ne'er returnest!

Chorus
No more, no more, no more returning,
In peace nor in war is he returning,
Till dawns the great day of doom and burning,
MacCrimmon is home, no more returning.

The breeze of the Bens is gently blowing,
The brooks in the glens are softly flowing;
Where boughs their darkest shades are throwing,
Birds mourn for thee who ne'er returnest!

Chorus

(Translated from Gaelic)

Francis Collinson points out in his book, *The Bagpipe*, that there seems to have been no time when piobaireachd was a simple form. In other words, it started life complicated. He suggests that it may have been 'converted' from the repertoire of another instrument, possibly the harp, whose music, according to tradition, was very complex. Sadly, no examples exist that can be confirmed as genuine remains of this ancient instrument's music, so no great significance can be attached to this theory. Recent research suggests, in any case, that piobaireachd may already have existed in a much more simple form before the MacCrimmons developed it.

It has already been mentioned that the Mac-Crimmons were hereditary pipers to the clan MacLeod (the post of clan piper was usually hereditary), but their skill and fame was such that they soon became teachers as well as practitioners. Donald Mor MacCrimmon opened a college of piping at Galtrigall in Skye, over the loch from Dunvegan Castle, which was the seat of the MacLeods, probably in the mid-seventeenth century. The college moved to Boreraig, a working farm, in the late seventeenth century, under the directorship of Patrick Og MacCrimmon, grandson of Donald Mor.

This became the mecca for all pipers, and where all clan chiefs sent young men to be trained, for a period of up to twelve years. It can be understood from this just how important was the post of piper and how difficult the business of playing pio-baireachd. The art, with its complexity, idiosyncrasies and alien sound, was not only restricted in numbers of enthusiasts, but demanded extremely intense and protracted periods of concentration on the part of both player and listener. According to Cedric Thorpe Davie in his *Scotland's Music*, the men who perfected this technique long ago were arrogant enough to believe that their pupils could not do better than imitate their teachers down to the very last detail, with perhaps just a suspicion of jealousy of the exceptionally gifted who might otherwise better their masters. From these beginnings, he goes on, came stagnation, which may only now be beginning to change, though in the face of much opposition from what he describes as 'the old guard'.

The MacCrimmons had their competitors. Charles MacArthur, one of the pupils of Patrick Og MacCrimmon, opened his own school, possibly at Ulva near Mull. Several piping schools were founded in the wake of the MacCrimmons', in fact, but these two were the principal ones, each developing their own particular, identifiable styles, which are preserved even today, although the colleges are long closed.

Before staff notation was introduced in the nineteenth century (that is, the technique of writing music down as notes on lines), pipe music was taught orally and a teacher would use a series of vocal sounds, or vocables, to 'sing' the music to his pupil, who would then copy exactly on his practice chanter, or *feadan*. This is still used today to help with rhythm and expression, where staff notation is not sufficient. The system was, and is, known as *canntaireachd*, and is also said to have been invented by the MacCrimmons. The vocables were committed to paper as follows, for example: *hiodroho, hodroho, haninen, hieachin*; and is even said to have been the inspiration for 'sol-fa' notation. Although the vocables were written down, they were not used to sight-read from, as is staff notation, they were used purely as a reminder to somebody already familiar with the tune. These days, staff notation and canntaireachd are used in conjunction with each other.

While no one can be absolutely certain who invented canntaireachd, it seems appropriate to allow the MacCrimmons the benefit of the doubt. Certainly, it was their private system from which the other piping schools later copied, although certain secrets about their system were always kept, rendering it still unintelligible, at least in part, even today.

Eventually, there were three systems of canntaireachd in use: the MacCrimmon, the MacArthur and the Nether Lorn (devised by the Campbell pipers). The last of these is the one which is still used by players of piobaireachd, as it has proved more intelligible than the MacCrimmon and has outlasted the MacArthur, of which no authentic example remains. No history of such a system for ceol beag (small music) is set down, although something similar is used, which has probably been adapted by modern pipers.

It is on record that Bonnie Prince Charlie had a particularly fine group of pipers as part of the army that attempted to win him the crown of Great Britain in 1745. However, as we all know, his dreams came to nought and he was forced to flee back to France.

The failure of the '45 Rebellion spelled danger for the bagpipes as well. At the trial of one James Reid, a piper for the Ogilvies, it was decided that the pipe was 'an instrument of war', as Highlanders seemed habitually to go into battle to its sound. Reid was executed and in 1746 the Disarming Act was brought into force. This forbade the carrying or hiding of arms and also the wearing of Highland dress in any form. Although the bagpipes were not mentioned specifically, they were deemed to be arms.

It is commonly supposed that this draconian Act was enforced to the letter, but though life certainly became much more difficult for the patriotic Scot, and many chiefs who had supported the Stuart restoration had their lands confiscated after the Rebellion and went abroad, pipers continued to be trained for at least another decade, though on a much smaller scale.

Coupled with this, however, was a growing fashion among those who still had land, to indulge in a more expensive 'southern-type' life-style than their meagre rents could cope with; for instance, sending their sons to public school in England. They were no longer willing, or able, to afford to keep up the old traditions and pipers were expendable items in the scheme of things. In the face of this massive loss of income and status, the colleges of piping buckled and they had all closed by the late eighteenth century.

It is safe to say that during this difficult period piping and the playing of piobaireachd did not die out. It is hard to say what would have happened, had it gone on for much longer than it did. Fortunately, William Pitt had the idea of raising the first Scottish regiments, for use on foreign battle-fields. Since the even less successful rebellion in 1715, there had been semi-official groups of Highlanders paid to keep vague order by hound-ing their fellow Highlanders, and these groups were now banded together to form official British fighting forces. The first of these was Mont-gomery's Highlanders, raised in 1757, which had thirty pipers and drummers attached to it; and others soon followed.

At this stage, only members of the regiments and the 'fencibles', who were to become the Territorial Army, technically, were allowed to play the pipes, but this did not deter a group of 'exiled' Scots in London forming the Highland Society, whose aim was to preserve the pipe music of the Highlands. They even considered setting up an academy of piping, an idea which came to nothing. Eventually, they decided on financing a yearly competition held at the Falkirk cattle-market for the playing of piobaireachd. Such a competition is still held annually in Inverness. The Disarming Act was repealed in 1782.

The MacCrimmons did not enter the compe-titions; their beloved college had been taken from them; their star was fading and perhaps the thought of competing against their own pupils in open battle as well was too much for their pride. One of their last pupils, however, John MacKay, won a great reputation for himself on this stage, and he and his son, Angus, carried on the great teaching traditions of the MacCrimmons.

In the early nineteenth century, the Highland Society began to encourage the writing down of piobaireachd in staff notation, by offering prizes for this. This, together with the use of tape-recorded playing, has rendered the art much more accessible to the ordinary musician.

During the nineteenth century, ceol mor was once again feared to be in decline, though it is hard to say if there was any justification for this opinion. At any rate, this view was held by the group of gentlemen pipers who formed the Piobaireachd Society in 1903. Their aims were to publish music, hold competitions and pay for instruction in piobaireachd. They achieved all these goals, but they kept such strict control that they almost snuffed out the whole venture. The problem centred on the nature of their rules, which had the Society arranging the competitions, publishing the music from which no deviation was allowed and then doing the judging as well. This led, ultimately, to dogmatism and an ever-decreasing number willing to put up with it. Reforms were made and the Society began to operate through the Northern Meeting, instead of holding their own competitions. This did improve matters but, as has already been discussed, something of the reactionary spirit remains to this day.

What most people listen to, of course, is 'small music': the march, the strathspey and reel, the jig; the music, in other words, of the pipe-bands. Francis Collinson laments their recent practice of neglecting traditional ceol beag music in favour of modern tunes often not even Scottish, far less bagpipe, in origin. This is not purely on nostalgic grounds, but principally because this has led to the pipes being played in a manner for which they are not designed. The nine-note scale of the pipes differs in crucial ways from the ordinary major scale, most noticeably in its very sharp D and its very flat G. This, and other features, can make harmonizing and playing with ordinary orchestral instruments, both of which are commonly done today, anathema to pipers, although both have achieved massive popularity among the public.

Though the Scottish regiments were the first to use pipes and drums together on a large scale, civilian bands were established in the late nineteenth century. Police forces have also taken up this particular gauntlet and now run some of the best bands in the world, winning many of the major international championships. One of the most successful of these is among the earliest of the police bands: Strathclyde Police Band, formerly Govan Police Pipe Band, formed in 1885, but even they have had to look to their laurels as there is now considerable competition from North America. The Canadians and Americans are extremely keen pipers and have, in addition, mastered piobaireachd.

The conventional minimum formula for a pipe-band is one bass-drummer, about four side-drummers and six pipers, although many bands are substantially larger than this. The pipers march in front, then comes the bass-drummer (sometimes flanked by two tenor-drummers) and finally the side-drummers. Heading them the magnificently garbed Drum Major complete with ceremonial mace, which is used to direct proceedings.

The musical director of a pipe-band is called the Pipe Major, who marches with the band in the front rank of the pipers, giving all signals if the Drum Major is not there. He is also responsible for tuning all the drones and chanters to the same pitch. Within the army, this job entails, in addition, the duty of instructing both band members and the officers of the regiment in the art of Highland dancing, in which a high standard is expected to be maintained. (George MacDonald Fraser's *The General Danced at Dawn* is an example, not necessarily typical, of how this all operates.)

AVERAGE SIZED PIPE BAND

S	S	S	S	} BASS SECTION
T		B	T	} PERCUSSION
P	P	P	P	}
P	P	P	P	} PIPE SECTION
P/M	P	P	P/S	}

D/M

D/M = Drum Major
P/M = Pipe Major
P/S = Pipe Sergeant
P = Pipers/Non-Commissioned Officers
T = Tenor Drummers
B = Bass Drummer
S = Side Drummer

More pipers and side drummers can be added: i.e. 16+pipers and 6+side drummers. Note: normally only 1 bass drummer and 2 tenor drummers per pipe band. More tenor and bass drummers can be added when massed bands are on parade.

The Drum Major makes all signals, such as music changes, formation of circles, changes in direction, and in the army, must be able to play the side-drum and the B Flat bugle, and have good knowledge of both tenor- and bass-drums. He shares responsibility, with the Pipe Major, for the general well-being of players and instruments.

These two are assisted by a Pipe Sergeant, a Drum Sergeant, and, in the army, a Pipe Corporal as well.

Finally, it will perhaps be of interest to the reader to know what the bagpipe looks like these days. A third drone was added at an unknown date, probably in the eighteenth century, but did not find immediate favour, and the one-, two- and three-drone pipes certainly co-existed for some time. The bag or *piob mor* is made of animal hide (usually sheep or horse) and is covered in tartan or velvet. This has five wooden tubes or 'stocks' tied into it, and from these lead the blowpipe, the two tenor and one bass drone, and the chanter. All these parts were at one time made from laburnum or holly wood, both indigenous to Scotland, but now African blackwood is the most popular material for this purpose. The bag is made of animal skin and is rubbed inside with honey, or some similar substance, in order to make it fully airtight and therefore efficient as an air reservoir; and also to absorb some of the moisture from the piper's breath. If moisture accumulates inside the drones and reeds, the instrument goes out of tune. The beauty of a tune played on the pipe, of course, is that the flow of music is continuous, which is not possible on any other wind instrument, unless the difficult technique of circular breathing is mastered. In order to accomplish this feat of non-stop music, the player has to learn to alternate between blowing into the bag through the blowpipe and squeezing it with his elbow, maintaining a steady pressure whichever he is doing, so as not to alter pitch.

All this may soon be a thing of the past, though. The latest fashion, and one that has been embraced by rock and folk groups, is the electronic bagpipe. This can be adjusted for pitch and volume and requires no blowing, as the bag contains a synthesizer and the chanter has contacts instead of holes, which are fingered in the usual way. The age of the electronic pipe-band may soon be upon us.

Fiddle

The fiddle, or violin, in the form familiar to us was perfected by the Italians in the sixteenth century and was certainly in use in Scotland by the early eighteenth century, and possibly a good deal earlier. For the beginnings of stringed instruments in Scotland, however, we have to go much further back.

There are three such instruments which were played with a bow: the *fedyl* (fiddle), the *rybid* (rebeck) and the *croud*. It is impossible to be exact about dates, but Melrose Abbey, started in 1136, provides us with a carving of a rebeck and Thomas the Rhymer (thirteenth century) mentions the first two in one of his poems. Evidence as to their origins is not clear, although they may both have been brought home by crusaders as early as the eleventh century. The third of these instruments, the croud, or gue as it was known in Shetland, may have been native to the Celtic countries of the British Isles (i.e. Wales, Ireland and Scotland) and is referred to in twelfth-century Arthurian and Ossianic ballads, when it was probably a plucked instrument.

It is important to remember that these early versions of the violin were a good deal cruder than the sophisticated instrument with which we are familiar today. It is recorded that Mary Queen of Scots, on hearing outside her window at Holyrood Palace a group of fiddle and rebeck players, who had come to pay their respects, hastily moved to another room. It is also said that John Knox, the fiercely puritanical Reformation minister, approved of this particular display, since the 'musicians' also sang psalms.

In the latter half of the sixteenth century, fiddlers fell on hard times. It is true, though, that anybody could put together a crude instrument and scrape away at a street corner for a few coins, and this became the gambit not only of 'vaga-bonds' but also of thieves and cut-throats, who took advantage of the kindly passer-by who opened his purse. Edinburgh's answer to this was to brand them on the cheek and banish them, if they could not show they were in the pay of an aristocrat or a burgh. Fiddlers (and bagpipers) were also, in the view of the Reformed Kirk, associated with witchery. It was, for example, revealed by the prosecution at the trial of Agnes Thomson in 1591 that she had danced a 'reill' to the sound of the fiddle. This is the first written record of a reel, which became the national dance of Scotland and is still very popular. Agnes Thomson was burnt.

All this adverse publicity prepared a very easy path for the viol, which was probably imported from France in the latter half of the sixteenth century. This instrument, much sweeter-toned than the fiddle, and with no nasty associations, was enjoyed by polite society and soon com-pletely swept aside its cruder counterpart. The viol was made in three sizes: the bass *viola da gamba*; the tenor *viola da braccio*; and the treble or descant viol. A 'chest' of viols was the usual collective noun for the set of six (two in each register) used for concerts, as the instruments were often stored in a purpose-built wooden chest. It must be emphasized, however, that although this instrument was occasionally used to play traditional music, and some Scots music was even composed specially for it, it was essentially a vehicle for classical music, and as such never became a folk instrument.

In the end, the viol was a kind of 'nine-day wonder' since it had gone out of fashion by the middle of the seventeenth century. What supplan-ted it was the violin, fresh from Italy, and a very different affair from the cacophonous fedyl. The first violins were made in Cremona by the Amati family in the sixteenth century, and though opinion varies as to when the first ones reached

Scotland, it seems likely that they were beginning to be familiar in the latter half of the seventeenth century.

Its versatility, and the precision with which notes could be placed, made the violin an extremely valued instrument, and very soon copies were being made in Scotland. As new models appeared from Italy, a Scots craftsman would reproduce it, advertising his work as a copy of that particular model.

It is important to record that there occurred at this stage a crossover between the folk and the classical traditions. Folk-fiddling, in other words, became fashionable, and the musician who entertained drawing-room society had to add Scots tunes to his basic repertoire of Haydn and Corelli. Later, musical societies made classical music accessible to ordinary folk, completing the circle.

The other important development was a surge of interest in dancing among the wealthy classes, in response to a visit to Edinburgh by the Duke and Duchess of York in 1680. Dancing, since the Church had forbidden the 'promiscuous' act of men and women dancing together in 1649, had been a somewhat clandestine activity. Now, in open defiance of an outraged clergy, the gentry danced reels, English country dances and minuets, to the sound of the fiddle.

This was the most important, and often only, instrument played where any public dancing took place, primarily because dancing-masters almost invariably played the dance-tunes at lessons on the fiddle, and dancers were more comfortable with a familiar sound when called upon to display their talents in a more formal setting. Depending on the amount of space available, the music would be provided by one or two fiddles, sometimes accompanied by a cello supplying a bass.

In 1723, twenty years after some trend-setters in Bath, the Edinburgh Assembly opened. This was a dancing-club, supposedly open to the general public, but in fact frequented only by 'persons of quality, and others of note', and which survived almost to the end of the century, with a gap for the '45 Rebellion. It also set a trend for the rest of the country to follow, since 'assemblies' began to spring up all over Scotland and dancing-masters took their talents to the provinces where, in addition to visiting the remote seats of the rural gentry, they began to teach larger classes of people slightly lower on the social scale, and no doubt for a more modest fee. Encouraged by this business-like attitude, the Scots took to dancing and, by the end of the century, it could no longer be claimed as a pastime only for the rich.

The development of the fiddle and its music was largely in the hands of educated people at this stage: of the school-teacher, of the dancing-master, of people interested in culture and the arts; a different story from that of other branches of folk-music. Many used to write down the tunes they were in the habit of playing in manuscript books, some of which have survived, and this led to commercial publishers taking an interest. The first of the printed collections of Scottish airs adapted for the use of the fiddle (and other instruments) was published by Henry Playford in 1700 (London). The names of the people who composed these tunes are lost to us for the most part; some bear the names of the dancing-masters who taught them and may have written the tunes; but, whoever they were, they formed the basis of the lively and continuing tradition we have inherited.

Thus far, no publication had appeared containing music designed specifically for the fiddle, but before moving on to these, mention must be made of James Oswald, born in Dunfermline around 1711. By 1736, he had made quite a reputation for himself in Edinburgh, and was earning a good living as a dancing-master, violinist, composer and organist. In 1743 he produced the *Caledonian Pocket Companion*, a collection of instrumental indigenous music which proved extremely popular. For the purposes of this section, Book III (1745) is notable for containing the first printing of a strathspey, a slow dance emanating, of course, from the Spey valley in Inverness-shire, and peculiarly associated with the fiddle, while the reel, on the other hand, was probably first danced to the bagpipes. This particular strathspey was composed by Oswald himself, as probably were other tunes in this volume originally thought to have come down the path of oral tradition.

The strathspey quickly became a firm favourite, along with reels and country dances, and this led to a spate of publications, including the first collection of purely fiddle music, entitled *Scots Reels or Country Dances*, published in Edinburgh by Robert Bremner (*circa* 1757), and *A Collection of Strathspeys or Old Highland Reels* by Angus Cumming (Edinburgh, 1780). The Cummings, who lived in Strathspey, were held in high regard for their grasp of the strathspey idiom, and were thought to have composed many themselves, but it is not certain if any Cumming compositions found their way into this publication.

In a revolutionary and influential volume, *The Art of Playing the Violin*, Geminiani advocated the practice of placing the chin on the left of the tailpiece, for a long time a highly controversial issue. This illustrates that the whole approach to playing the fiddle was becoming much more sophisticated.

It is time to draw attention to one or two of the most famous exponents of this art. Not many references exist to men who achieved recognition by playing the fedyl and indeed, in view of them and their instrument's reputation, it would be more appropriate to attach the 'infamous' to their achievements. Such a description might be apt for Patie Birnie, who lived in Kinghorn in Fife either in the seventeenth or eighteenth century, and made his living by playing to passengers as they disembarked from the Leith-Kinghorn ferries, whether or not they wished to be entertained, and then asking them for the price of a drink. He is credited with having written the words and the music to 'The Auld Man's Mare's Dead' and even had a poem written about him by Allan Ramsay, albeit somewhat frank in nature, of which this is an extract:

> When strangers landed, wow sae thrang
> Fuffin and peghin he wad gang
> And crave their pardon that sae lang
> He'd been a-comin;
> Syne out his bread-winner out he'd bang
> And fa' tae bummin.

thrang – throng; *fuffin* – puffing; *peghin* – panting; *bread-winner* – his fiddle; *to bang out* – to bring out quickly; *bummin* – playing badly

One of the most newsworthy early fiddlers was James Macpherson, who was hanged in 1700. His mother was a gipsy and his father was the Laird of Invereshie – they were not married. His father, however, gave him a home until he (the Laird) died, after which his mother reclaimed him. James apparently grew up extremely intelligent and with a great gift for fiddling; he also headed a band of robbers, who were said to have an aversion to any kind of violence. In due course, this outlaw band were arrested, tried and condemned to be hanged. A rescue was effected and Macpherson and his men escaped, only to be captured once again after only a short spell of freedom. This time, there was to be no escape for Macpherson, though it is said that a reprieve was on its way while his execution was taking place.

While he was waiting in the condemned cell, it is claimed that he wrote his only surviving tune, 'Macpherson's Rant', which he was then allowed to play on the scaffold as a last privilege. Upon finishing the tune, he is said to have offered his fiddle to the crowd, and when no one was brave enough to come forward, he smashed the fiddle over his knee in disgust. Eventually, the pieces found their way to the Macpherson Clan House Museum at Newtonmore. It is actually unconfirmed that he was even a fiddler, far less a composer, since such records as there are may have confused him with one of his band, who

apparently played the viol, but readers will agree
that it is a wonderful story. Robert Burns, in fact,
was so taken with it that he wrote some words to
the tune:

> Fareweel, ye dungeons, dark and strong,
> The wretch's destinie!
> Macpherson's time will not be long
> On yonder gallows-tree.
>
> Sae rantingly, sae wantonly,
> Sae dauntingly gaed he
> He played a spring, and danced it round,
> Below the gallows-tree.

Niel Gow was undoubtedly one of the greatest
of Scotland's fiddlers. He was born into a family of
weavers at Inver in Perthshire in 1727, and lived
there all his life, refusing to move to any of the
centres where his music was so much in demand.

He was also the first of a new breed of fully professional fiddlers, who was able to earn a proper living from his art as a result of the huge increase of interest in folk-music by the wealthy classes, both north and south of the border.

He was largely self-taught, and by the time he won a national fiddling competition at Glenfinnan in 1745 he had already established quite a reputation for himself. After this, he gained the patronage of the Duke of Atholl, who had him play at all the grand social events and took him to London, where he created a sensation. Thereafter, and for the next forty years or more, he was quite literally a *sine qua non* at all parties of any distinction, since these events would be arranged to suit his timetable. It is said that he would electrify the dancers by giving sudden shouts during his playing, whereupon the people on the floor would redouble their exertions. He became a skilful exponent of the rather sudden up-bow stroke which gives the strathspey its distinctive rhythm, or 'Scots snap', and which has caused trouble even to Sir Yehudi Menuhin.

In addition to his startling success as a fiddler, he was also a considerable and prolific composer, and although he created doubts about this by modestly hesitating to acknowledge his work, it is

now certain that he added some seventy tunes to the repertoire. These, of course, included dance-music, such as hornpipes, jigs, reels and strathspeys, but he also composed music to listen to, among which were the slow strathspeys, played in an exaggeratedly staccato manner. One of his most famous pieces, a slow air, was 'Niel Gow's Lament for the Death of His Second Wife'.

Niel Gow was a firm believer in the equality of men, and never fawned upon the high-ranking people for whom he performed. For this and his personal integrity he was respected and even popular. Confident in this happy state of affairs, he was able to take a few liberties – one story tells us that he was listening to the daughter of a duchess playing the piano and remarked, 'That lassie o' yours, my lady, has a gude ear.' A sycophantic gentlemen guest questioned the use of the term 'lassie', whereupon Gow is said to have retorted, 'What would I ca' her? I never heard she was a laddie.'

All of Niel Gow's four sons were musical, but the one who became best known was the youngest, Nathaniel. He learned to play the cello and trumpet as well as the fiddle, developing classical and traditional tastes, and became one of the trumpeters of King George IV in Scotland. He took over the leadership of an Edinburgh dance-band from his brother William when he died, which became as famous and as much in demand as his father's.

In 1796, he started a music-publishing business, producing general music as well as the compositions of his father, his brothers and himself, which continued until 1823 when his son, Niel junior, also a composer and a skilful amateur musician, died. Unhappily, this venture had not been a great success and Nathaniel had all his property confiscated for debts. Nathaniel himself died in 1831.

It seems a pity that their story should end on such a sad note, for the Gows were undoubtedly a remarkable family and were a considerable influence on the national musical scene for nearly one hundred years.

The Gows, however, did not operate a mono-poly, for there were other fiddler composers of note living at the same time. Of these, perhaps the greatest was William Marshall, born at Fochabers in 1748. Like Niel Gow, he did not come from a wealthy family and went into service with the Duke of Gordon at the age of twelve, under whose patronage he remained until his death in 1833. He had had only six months' schooling at twelve years old, and, with his new-found advantages, set about improving his knowledge of the world, eventually becoming a mathematician, mechanic and even architect. His first love, however, was music, and encouraged by the Duke, he com-posed and published two collections during his lifetime. The second of these, which appeared in 1822, is thought to be among the finest Scottish fiddle music ever printed, and made high techni-cal demands on the player. He wrote a number of the slow strathspey-type air for which Niel Gow was so famous, and it is possible that he actually invented this form.

Others who made their names and their livings from composing and playing the fiddle include Angus Cumming (of strathspey fame), Isaac Cooper, John Bowie and Robert Petrie, all of whom brought out collections of reels and strathspeys during this rich period. The most prolific of them all, however, and the last of the famous Scots fiddle composers, was James Scott Skinner (1843–1927).

Skinner was born in Banchory, Aberdeenshire, and, like Gow and Marshall, did not come from a wealthy family. His father was a gardener, who was forced to give this up when he lost some of the fingers on one hand. Undaunted by this, he turned to his hobby as a source of income and became a dancing-master, holding his fiddle in his right hand and strapping the bow to his damaged left.

James and his brother learned to play the fiddle as well, and after their father died, earned money by playing at dances. Ultimately, James became a dancing-master like his father, adopting 'Scott' as a middle name out of respect for his teacher William Scott of Stoneywood. He made a success of this and was invited to teach the tenantry at Balmoral, where he became firm friends with Queen Victoria's famous gillie, John Brown. Soon he had widened his area of teaching to the whole of the north of Scotland, but by this time he was becoming dissatisfied with teaching, and wanted to abandon this in favour of performing. He had, like others before him, been giving the occasional public performance, but now he was to become the first full-time professional concert fiddler. Before long he was famous all over the country, and openly acknowledged his regrets at having spent so many frustrating years teaching.

He was a gifted composer, too, writing some-times highly complex pieces, which could really only be performed by someone with at least some classical training; he admitted that he could not bear to listen to fiddlers who had had only a rough training. He was also extremely prolific, with 600 pieces printed and probably many more still in manuscript. Perhaps his most famous tunes are 'Cradle Song' and 'The Bonny Lass o' Bon Accord', but he himself was particularly fond of strath-speys, composing many and bestowing on himself the title 'the Strathspey King'.

Above all, he was deeply and passionately committed to his art, and even at the height of his fame, still gave one-off lessons to hundreds of hopeful admirers who queued to see him. His technique was made available to thousands more, though, as he was the first Scottish fiddler to be recorded on disc, becoming something of a media personality. It was during his lifetime, and with the advent of recording technology, that solo fiddling became mainly music to listen to, rather than to dance to, something that persists to this day. Skinner kept up a punishing concert schedule right into his eighties, playing at least thirty-six concerts, including the Albert Hall, when he was eighty-one.

The dance-band tradition made so popular by Niel Gow and others continued, but in a slightly different form. In its modern incarnation, the main instrument became the accordion, with the fiddle, drums, piano, double bass and occasionally cornet, providing the accompaniment. This format was first adopted by Jimmy Shand in the 1920s, whose band made the first of their extremely popular radio broadcasts in the 1930s, but the hundreds of dance-bands which sprang up in his wake adapted this formula to suit. They suffered something of a decline in fortunes in the 1960s, but they do remain popular, with radio programmes such as *Take the Floor* and *Pure Scotch* continuing the tradition.

The fiddling tradition of the Shetland Isles is altogether different from that of mainland Scotland. The main reason for this is the strong links these hundred or so islands have with Scandinavia. Until the fifteenth century, they were actually part of Scandinavia, but were pledged to Scotland in 1469 as part of a marriage settlement for Princess Margaret of Norway. The pledge was not redeemed, and the islands were annexed to Scotland in 1612. Naturally, the people living there did not immediately give up their traditions in favour of those of Scotland, and strong political, cultural and trading links were maintained with Norway for some 200 years after that. The Norse language, too, lingered until the middle of the eighteenth century. Some present-day Shetlanders still feel much more closely tied with Scandinavia than with Scotland.

It is thought that the modern violin (the Amati violin developed in Italy in the sixteenth century) may have arrived in Shetland at the beginning of the eighteenth century, brought by Dutch fishermen, or possibly Shetland seamen returning home. A stringed instrument, called a gue, which was similar to the violin, was being played in Shetland before this, so the violin was brought to a receptive and familiar audience. Not a great deal is known about the gue, except that it was rather a crude affair, consisting of a box across which were stretched a couple of horsehairs and may have been played like a cello. The violin, one feels, must have been a welcome replacement.

Statistical accounts of the eighteenth century show that Shetlanders were extremely fond of music and dancing, as indeed they still are. The fiddle was without doubt the most important instrument of the isles until the accordion and the piano began to find favour in the twentieth century. Almost every man could play the fiddle and good fiddlers were held in great esteem, playing at most important occasions, and especially at weddings.

Even today, but more and more rarely, the fiddler enacts a special ritual before and around a wedding. The bridegroom issues a formal invitation to the chosen principal fiddler, who first of all plays at a 'sealing of the bargain' dance at the bride's house. His next important task is to lead the bridal party to and from the church; finally he plays at the reception dance. In some places, the bride was ceremonially put to bed by a party which included the fiddler, but this custom is now obsolete, much to the relief, doubtless, of new brides.

The Shetland tradition is, like all the idioms discussed in this book, an oral one – the earliest Shetland music to be found in staff notation is mid-nineteenth century – and each fiddler would have his own slightly different way of playing the traditional tunes and evenings would be spent comparing versions. Even today, when music is printed and there are cassettes and records available, there is resistance to allowing one particular version to prevail.

There are certain terms used to describe the indigenous repertoire, but these do not cover the whole of it and are, in any case, confusing since the labelling can be inconsistent. The main categories, however, are Muckle, or Aald, reels; Shetland reels; trowie tunes; Greenland or whaling tunes; Yakki tunes; and wedding tunes. The Muckle reel is now obsolete as a dance, but is preserved as listening music in some fiddlers' repertoires. The tunes are very old and are said to bear a strong resemblance to Norwegian 'Hallings' or country dances, among the oldest dance-tunes in the Hardanger fiddle tradition. Shetland reel tunes are still commonly played in the Shetlands, principally because they have been adapted to fit modern requirements. They may at one time have been more jig-like in rhythm, and are said still to be Scandinavian in character. They are played in simple duple time, to be used interchangeably with the reel-tunes of mainland Scotland. The growing popularity of Scottish reels in eighteenth-century Shetland led to the demise of the Shetland reel as a dance, but the incoming tunes were so successfully Shetlandized that it became impossible in some cases to tell if a tune was traditional Shetland or one that had been adapted. Trowie tunes are fairy tunes; this label is supposed to show that the composer got his inspiration while under the inflenuce of the fairies. The cynic might suggest that the word 'fairy' is a euphemism for something a little less nebulous in character. 'Greenland' or 'whaling' tunes speak for themselves. There are no surviving 'Yakki' tunes, but this was the name given to tunes learned from the Eskimos by Orkney and Shetland whaling men. Weddings have already been covered.

Until the beginning of this century, lack of good communications, both by sea to the islands and by road on the islands, made self-contained entertainment vital. On a winter's night without television, radio or record-player, the time could be spent listening to a fiddler. Ten years into the 1900s saw the islanders with pianos, concertinas and guitars, and beginning to build community halls. It was time for the fiddle to adapt or disappear: the solo fiddle could not be heard in the larger settings and the islanders, in any case, were being seduced by the sounds of the outside world. The fiddle became part of a dance-band, which would play waltzes and quadrilles as well as traditional dance-music. In the face of this limitless competition, interest in things local began to take second place, with traditional music becoming more and more something to listen to, returning to the setting for which it was designed, the home.

This is not to say, however, that Shetland fiddling was shut away in a cupboard, never again to emerge into the public eye. Proof of this maintained enthusiasm manifested itself in the forming of the Shetland Folk Society in 1947, when Tom Anderson was asked to lead its folk fiddle band in performing a repertoire of indigenous music. This led, in due course, to his founding of the Shetland Fiddlers' Society in 1960, which still flourishes. Tom Anderson has been instrumental in the revitalization of Shetland fiddle music, and was awarded the MBE in 1977 for his services in this cause. It is a good thing to be able to report that the Shetland fiddle tradition has survived so well; the accordion and fiddle clubs of Lerwick have large attendance figures, attracting young people who might be discouraged by the rather more conservative reputation of the Shetland Fiddlers' Society. Like most survivors from another age, though, a price has had to be paid, and modern composers and performers of Shetland music admit that the native dialect has become submerged in favour of a rather more standard Scottish sound. The repertoire of accordion and fiddle clubs now includes country and western music, which is extremely popular. The whole effect is rather smoother than the traditional harder sound, which younger people often reject for this reason. The arrival of staff notation, too, has been a mixed blessing, since the discipline of learning this in a formal, competitive setting (i.e. in school), may have put off some potential fiddlers. The beauty of an oral tradition is that technique is assimilated gradually, through listening to and copying a familiar group of tunes. Tuition is minimal and the whole process is barely noticeable.

The old tunes continue to be played, though, and recording equipment makes the spread of music and technique easier. This, in itself, is enough to perpetuate the oral method of learning, which may, after all, have something to recommend it.

Modern Times

Whatever its correct title, it is important to realize that the so-called modern revival has not happened in a vacuum; it is part of a continuous process, and trying to pinpoint a starting date is like trying to gauge when the Industrial Revolution began. What distinguishes this particular revival is a merging of interest, so to speak; a final acknowledgment that it is all right for everybody, whoever they are, to be interested in folk-music and to meet in the same places to listen to and perform it. Formerly, as we have seen, while the polite classes showed interest in what was considered rather vulgar and low-class music, they tended to indulge it on their own terms: suitably adapted for refined ears and performed, in the drawing-room, only by those who passed the test of respectability. All this, of course, did no more than reflect general behaviour patterns.

Among those who have had most influence on traditional music in the second half of the twentieth century, naturally, are the immediate precursors of today's folk musicians. Cecil Sharp (1859–1924), in England, with his assiduous song-collecting, played a very important part in stimulating interest, especially in bringing traditional music into the school curriculum, though his versions tended to continue the trend of adaptation, rather than preservation of original material. Gustav Holst and Ralph Vaughan Williams, also, were keen to promote the cause, and wrote many very beautiful arrangements of tradtional tunes. In Scotland, Gavin Greig and James Duncan (school-teacher and minister respectively), collected over 3000 song versions from Aberdeenshire and neighbouring counties, which has proved invaluable to later enthusiasts.

In the Highlands, Marjory Kennedy Fraser was busy recording Gaelic music on the phonograph and Frances Tolmie, a native Gaelic speaker, was noting down the songs she heard sung round about her in Skye. Others equally enthusiastic about preserving Gaelic culture were Calum Maclean and John Lorne Campbell with his wife Margaret Fay Shaw. Together with the starting of the National Mod in 1892 and the springing up of all kinds of musical societies and clubs, there was plenty of enthusiasm for music, but not necessarily for performing or listening to it in its unadulterated form. Those who were keen on 'true' traditional music, both song and instrumental, were in a minority, and the bulk of Scottish music available to the public at this time was what Francis Collinson would class as national music, i.e. written expressly for publication. Much of this is very good, but, sadly, a substantial proportion of it falls, at best, into the category of banal and, at worst, is embarrassingly sentimental. Inexplicably, this was and remains popular, especially among nostalgic expatriates.

The scene was set for a reaction against this distorted image of Scotland and when intimations of contemporary American folk-music began to reach Britain by way of radio broadcast and record there was considerable interest. Here was something new and exciting, a record of everyday events taking place in the industrial present – songs of working people: rail-road workers, miners, lorry-drivers; it also signalled the start of the wide-spread use of the acoustic guitar as a folk instrument. The gradual marrying of these work-songs with jazz rhythms became known as 'skiffle' which achieved brief but spectacular success during the fifties. This was urban man finally finding his voice and he found a hugely receptive audience in Britain. Over the following years, programmes of these songs were broadcast on the radio, performed and presented for the first time by those who lived the life the songs described. It was a new concept: no longer were the polished tones of classically trained singers heard performing equally polished arrangements; instead, unelocuted, regional accents sang the harsh realities of industrial life, and later on the protest songs of the sixties. It was a revolution.

A revolution has to have its heroes, and one of these duly emerged in the shape of Ewan MacColl (1915–89). He was born Jimmy Miller in the industrial north of England of Scottish parents; his father had lost his job in Scotland because of his trade union activities and moved to Salford in Lancashire. This cultural dichotomy was the basis of his justification for singing English and Scottish versions of folk-songs, while energetically asserting that singers should remain true to their background by performing indigenous songs in their own accents.

He changed his name to Ewan MacColl in 1945, when he set up Theatre Workshop in Manchester with his long-time colleague, Joan Littlewood, and broadened his influence on the arts scene.

During a career which spanned over fifty years he wrote many political songs, commenting on and observing the nature of the working man's life, and sang them with fierce sincerity. This rather serious attitude later led him to reject the 'mid-Atlantic' anonymity which became the hallmark of an over-commercialized skiffle movement. He was also one of the pioneers of the radio broadcasts which brought this music to the listening public at large for the first time. Of these, the most famous were *Singing the Fishing*, which won the *Prix d'Italia* (1960) and *The Travelling People* (1964). These broadcasts, which won him and his producer Charles Parker such acclaim, did not, however, only represent the new 'industrial' music which had become so popular in America, but also encompassed the old traditional songs and ballads. MacColl had a remarkable knowledge and love of these, his interest stimulated by his musical parents, and this led to prolific publishing and recording, including printed collections like *Scotland Sings*, *The Singing Island* and *The Long Harvest*.

One is tempted to speak of eras ending with the death of a notable figure in any field, but the best tribute that can be paid to Ewan MacColl is that the era of folk-music has not ended; it lives on. This is in no small way due to his personal energy and his philosophy that folk-music should be dynamic and responsive to the needs and issues of the day, as well as respectful of past achievements.

Another important event in the story of the revival was the opening of the School of Scottish Studies in Edinburgh in 1951. Here, for the first time, was the notion of treating traditional culture of all kinds as a subject for serious academic study, worthy of an official place within the University of Edinburgh. One of the first people to undertake research in the modest accommodation the School first occupied has been mentioned in this book already: Francis Collinson. There was also Hamish Henderson, a man already respected for his work in the field, and whose reputation has increased with the years.

The School's remit was to pursue the strands of every aspect of Scottish culture and create an archive encompassing social history, anthropology, archaeology, folk-tales and place names as well as traditional Scots and Gaelic music. All of these, but particularly the last, since so much of the material has been derived from oral sources from schools to fishing boats, have included a vast amount of recorded material, which now amounts to more than 5000 hours. The School became a department in the Faculty of Arts in 1965, later introducing undergraduate courses, and despite criticism in recent years that materials housed in the archive were not easily enough available to performing musicians, continues to develop and extend its work.

Academic study, however, is not how most of those interested in folk-music want to spend their evenings. For them, nothing could be nicer than passing time in the company of others similarly inclined, whether performing or listening. For this purpose, the folk club is ideal and this phenomenon, too, plays an important part in this story, and made its first appearance under this title in the wake of the highly successful People's Festivals.

Most people have heard of the Edinburgh International Festival, which started in 1947. It quickly gained a deservedly good reputation but was condemned in equally strong terms for adopting an elitist attitude. For although the Festival did stage programmes of 'folk'-music, they were rather in the Victorian parlour mould, which was hardly likely to satisfy lovers of the new, more 'real' approach. For this reason, the first People's Festival was held in 1951. In the end, only five of these took place, between 1951 and 1955, but the spirit which gave birth to them lives on in the Edinburgh Festival Fringe and the Edinburgh Folk Festival itself.

It also lives on in folk clubs. Of course, 'folk club' is simply another name for the original ceilidh – a meeting of people in an informal setting, who perform and/or listen to traditional music. The difference this time was that, encouraged by the American example to search out their own culture, the youth of Scotland was turning to traditional music *en masse*. There was also a distinction made between 'source' musicians and 'revivalists', the former performing music handed down in the oral tradition and the latter music learned from printed or recorded sources. The overlap between these two categories makes this distinction more and more academic with the passing decades. Folk clubs and societies sprang up all over Scotland and it was during this period of the late fifties and early sixties that many of the musicians who are still performing today made their debuts: Jean Redpath, Archie Ray and Cilla Fisher and Jimmie Macgregor are but a few examples. Jeannie Robertson, who died in 1975, was to many the best of all of them. She was discovered in 1953 and was immediately success-ful, captivating her audiences with her warmth and charm, and thrilling them with her marvellous voice and faultless musicianship. She had a huge repertoire, which, as well as traditional ballads, lyric songs and children's songs, included a vast reservoir of tales. In 1968, she was awarded the MBE.

Jeannie Robertson fitted well into a world that was beginning to see barriers broken down: she was born into a family of travellers, and although she ultimately settled down in Aberdeen, she never disowned her heritage and did much to improve the rather appalling image her fellows had. She was a valuable medium through whom the different cultures could communicate and the wealth of traditional knowledge the travelling people had to offer an interested world could be discovered.

Travellers, or tinkers, have a very long history indeed. They were an ancient 'tribe' of craftsmen who moved about the country working when they needed to, and performing a useful function for farmers who needed periodic help for various manual tasks. In exchange, they would be allowed to camp and often to poach a bit of game. This attitude of compromise was not shared by most other members of the community, who did not have a mercantile interest in the tinkers. By them, the tinkers were reviled as lazy, dirty, ill-educated and dishonest – people who had no permanent home and worked only when they had to. Not unexpectedly, their way of life, coupled with the relentless barrage of criticism and vilification, has affected their artistic expression, which was described by Ewan MacColl as having a 'heroic quality', full of impassioned defiance against a hostile world and self-assertion of its own. Moving constantly from place to place, they would pick up odds and ends of all kinds of music and lore, which they imbued with their own style and added to their stock of native traveller culture.

The revival discovered the travellers in the shape of Jeannie Robertson and others such as Belle Stewart and Betsy Whyte. The relationship burgeoned, not a little due to the remarkable efforts of Hamish Henderson, who made considerable efforts to forge friendships, often travelling and camping with the people in whose songs and stories he was interested. A naturally articulate and expressive people, their confidence grew in the warmth of his approach. Slowly, cautious tentacles were extended and grasped the opportunity presented to make a unique contribution to the folk-music scene. These initial contacts made, the travellers' progress was not impeded, and in the years since then, they have been regular and lauded performers at most of the major folk festivals and clubs. Such has been their success, in fact, that the Scottish Travellers' Council, which represents the interests of the travellers, has made plans to set up a Scottish Gipsy Festival to be a focal point for all traveller culture, but also providing another platform for traditional artists generally. The town of Blairgowrie, a long-time favourite gathering-place for travellers, hosted annual festivals in the sixties, but eventually abandoned them at a time when feelings against the itinerant population were running high. Recently, the town started to mount a festival again in conjunction with the Tourist Board, a sign, perhaps, of a general growing acceptance of travelling people, but have sadly rejected plans for future festivals, though not, apparently, on the grounds of anti-traveller feeling. The following song 'The Yellow on the Broom', was written for Betsy Whyte:

Chorus
I ken ye dinna like it lass, tae winter in the toon,
For the scaldies aye miscry us, and they try tae bring us doon,
An' it's hard tae raise the three bairns in a single flea-box room,
But I'll tak ye on the road again, when the yellow's on the broom.

The scaldies ca' us tinker dirt and sconse oor bairns in school
But who cares what a scaldie thinks for a scaldie's but a fool
They never hear the yorlin's sang nor see the flax in bloom
For they're aye cooped up in hooses when the yellow's on the broom.

Chorus

Nae sale for pegs or baskets noo, so jist tae stay alive
We've had tae work at scaldie jobs fae nine o'clock till five,
But we ca' nae man oor maister, for we own the warld's room
An' we'll bid fareweel tae Brechin when the yellow's on the broom.

Chorus

I'm weary for the springtime when we tak the road yince mair
Tae the plantin an' the pearlin an' the berryfields at Blair
When we meet up wi' oor kinfolk fae a' the country roon
An' the gaun-aboot folk tak the road when the yellow's on the broom.

Chorus

scaldie – travellers' word for people who do not travel; *sconse* – cheat; *yorlin* – yellow-hammer; *pearlin* – pearling

The reader will have noticed no mention yet of any modern revival of Gaelic music, but this, too, received its share of attention, though at a later stage. Of course, there was the National Mod, set up by An Comunn Gaidhealach as part of a general scheme to regenerate interest in the language. This had, since its inception in 1892, been encouraging Gaelic singing, but it had always been a rather contrived affair, with choirs singing in harmony (an alien concept in Gaeldom) or trained soloists (another alien concept) all performing music written by outsiders who could neither speak Gaelic, nor grasp the subtleties peculiar to the music. The minute amount of air time allocated to Gaelic by the BBC broadcasted this style as the most acceptable. In more recent years, the accent in the Mod has begun to change: more importance is now placed on the traditional manner of singing, and the introduction of a competition for folk groups has proved to be a valuable vehicle for sheer exposure time of Gaelic material.

The School of Scottish Studies has also played its part, along with the Folklore Institute of Scotland and the Linguistic Survey of Scotland, in encouraging interest in Gaelic, by collecting and recording material. The short-lived People's Festival, too, invited, among others, Flora MacNeil from Barra to perform, who was one of the first modern musicians to specialize in traditional unaccompanied Gaelic singing and to perform for a wider public.

All this represented a perceptible, but very slow, change in attitudes. When Gaelic-speaking people were at long last released from their isolation by the advent of better communications, they suffered a true culture shock. With a much broader horizon suddenly presented to them, it is perhaps not surprising that their attention was temporarily diverted from the path of their own traditions; and the demonstrable falling-off of their interest did not encourage outsiders to help them preserve their heritage either. In this, Scotland compared particularly badly with other Celtic countries (Wales, Ireland and France), even to the extent of actively discouraging the use of Gaelic at school by children who learned it as their first language at home. As the language suffered, so did the music, and Gaels quickly responded to skiffle, pop and country and western.

School has undoubtedly a huge influence, whether good or bad, on the formative years of young people. Neglect or indifference on the part of teachers, or education authorities, leads to the same attitude in many children, and this is precisely what plagued (and still plagues) the field of traditional music. While the world at large was beginning to appreciate the old skills again, the world of education was doing nothing to supply this demand. There were simply no teachers who were willing or able to undertake the job, since the decision-makers had come to the conclusion that the traditional arts had no value educationally. The report published as recently as 1984 by the Scottish Arts Council on this subject referred specifically to a music adviser who was told during training to cut out all 'Scottishness'. Apart from certain enlightened teachers who used their spare time to form folk clubs, notably Morris Blythman, whose 1950s experiment at Allan Glen's School in Glasgow was such a success that Hamish Henderson himself came there to record material, this has remained the case. It is only in very recent years, for instance, that any of the formal examination syllabi has encompassed traditional music, and the Council records its concern that, because of a continuing lack of properly qualified staff (and public expenditure cuts), the nettle will remain largely ungrasped.

This concern is echoed in an essay by Ailie Munro in *Folk-music in School*, who sees an important role for traditional music in education, judging by her own experiments in the sixties. These were conducted at schools in 'tough' areas of Glasgow, where she found that children classified as virtually ineducable responded well to songs, especially when they had words that were appealing. Her discovery that of folk, art and pop-music the last found most favour with the children is not a surprise, but there was an encouraging interest in folk-music, which she felt could help teach children important values. She observes that folk-song, unlike the other two, is accessible to people of any age or rank and indeed positively endorses egalitarian principles. It is also accessible to those who have not achieved a particularly high standard of musicianship. As Ailie Munro says in her essay, 'Pop-music is the most pervasive influence on the majority of young teenagers, and pop has some doubtful effects; art-music is distant and unfamiliar and requires a bridging of the gulf; folk-music not only can help to provide that bridge, but is not too difficult to involve the children in, for its own sake, and with good results for their development towards adult life.' This essay was written in 1978, but the thrust of it remains as true today as it was then. Some progress has been made: teachers do now ask traditional musicians to come and perform at their schools, as with the visits of Cilla Fisher and Artie Trezise, with their act 'The Singing Kettle', to primary schools in central Scotland; a Helensburgh school is now offering a scholarship in traditional music; some teachers, acknowledging the 'cross-fertilization' that has occurred between traditional music, jazz, and now rock, use these examples to appeal to their teenage pupils (one instance of this was when the teacher used the version of 'Loch Lomond' made popular by the Gaelic folk-rock group, Runrig, and worked backwards to the original manifestation); and there has been remarkable success achieved in the Shetland Isles with the schools' programme of Shetland fiddle playing, run almost single-handedly by Tom Anderson, now in his eighties. But the Arts Council report in 1984 showed very variable attitudes on the part of local authorities to the question of the teaching of traditional music, and a general lack of resources even if an authority had a positive attitude. The Council admits there is little evidence of a radical change since then.

According to Peter Cooke, in his essay 'Music-learning in Traditional Societies', an entirely different approach must be adopted to the whole notion of teaching music to schoolchildren. He

75

uses the example of a house ceilidh (rather than the more formal 'concert' version) as a possible model for consideration, where people meet in order to enjoy music. There is no requirement for people to perform if they are not in the mood, and those who want to perform are encouraged to do so, no matter what their standard is. Here, therefore, is an excellent learning atmosphere for young singers or instrumentalists; they have ample opportunity to study what their elders are doing, in a relaxed and uncoercive environment; they can join in if they feel like it, or go home to experiment on their own, with the occasional piece of advice from an adult. Gradually, technique and repertoire are assimilated, with minimum stress and distress. Compare this with the average approach adopted in schools, which many readers will doubtless recall. The class is herded into a room and music is 'done' by everybody, with no real choices being offered, and no opportunity just to sit and listen, if that is what a child would prefer to do.

Too much emphasis, Peter Cooke says, is placed on the importance of staff notation; some children might feel more drawn to music if they did not have to grapple with the complexities of reading key signatures and notes off a page, and were instead encouraged to learn purely by ear (this is, in fact, a common approach adopted in primary schools). Those who have a gift for music are very fortunate, and should be encouraged; but then so should the less gifted, who in the school setting can often be made to feel completely inadequate and unable to offer anything musically. This is clearly wrong, if only because making music is so enjoyable in an uninhibited environment. At a ceilidh, no one is forced to do anything they do not want to, but will always be given an opportunity to perform. Cooke acknowledges the potential difficulties in adopting this approach in schools, but makes some proposals, including the idea of abandoning the formal class music lesson altogether, in favour of an optional 'club' attended by pupils of all ages and where older pupils would themselves have the opportunity of teaching.

Although the picture in schools is not all it might be, school is not the only place to learn about traditional music, and during the sixties and seventies it became increasingly obvious that the resurgence of interest in the traditional arts was no 'flash in the pan'. As more and more clubs and societies were formed to further their interests, more and more names were made, such as the Corries, Aly Bain and Barbara Dickson (now famous for quite another kind of singing and who first sprang to prominence in the sixties, when she performed with Archie Fisher); and the media, especially the BBC, took more interest. In 1966 the Traditional Music and Song Association of Scotland (TMSA) was formed, whose aims were to promote the indigenous arts in every way. This it did, and still does, by organizing festivals, concerts and ceilidhs throughout the country and encouraging the collection and publication of traditional music. The efforts of this group have been greatly praised, particularly as their festivals have managed to attract an admirable mixture of the famous and the not-so-famous to participate in workshops and in much informal music-making as well as the competitions. Their energies have been devoted to the whole range of the indigenous arts, including whistling, diddling, mouth organ and Jew's-harp, as well as the more 'usual' skills, making their events quite fascinating to attend. Most of this tremendous work has been done on sheer good-will – their first paid national organizer was only appointed in 1987, as a direct result of the recommendations made in the Arts Council 1984 report.

As well as producing their first recording on their own label recently (The Working Year), they have started a new youth project, based in Tayside Region, where it is hoped that its steering group will bring together young people interested in learning about traditional music, and provide a centre for local musicians and others as well as a model for other areas. They also plan to adopt national championship competitions, in order to

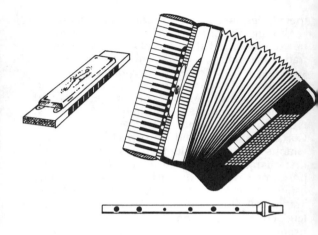

stimulate enthusiasm among young musicians and possibly to encourage the notion of a touring folk ensemble, taking a leaf out of Ireland's book, where Comhaltas Ceoltoiri Eireann (the Irish equivalent of An Comunn Gaidhealach) have had enormous success touring Irish traditional musicians through Britain and America.

In response to efforts like this, young people began to embrace their newly rediscovered culture, and the waiting lists of private teachers and groups such as the Clarsach Society, the College of Piping, the Royal Scottish Pipe Band Association and the various fiddle and accordion clubs grew steadily.

The revival probably reached its peak in the sixties and early seventies, but though the graph has levelled out, interest remains high. The activities of PERFORM (Performance of Folk and Other Related Music), set up in 1981 to help the cause of traditional music all over Britain, have helped to ensure the media's attention is brought to the folk scene. Newspapers now give far more coverage to traditional music, printing both features and programmes of events; and much more traditional music is now being broadcast on the radio and television. Though the quality of these programmes varies, many of them are first-rate. Radio seems to offer the best of these, in *The Music Makers* (no longer broadcast), *Travelling Folk* and *A Measure of Scots* for example, and in magazine programmes such as *Macgregor's Gathering*. The Arts Council report was particularly concerned that the media are not always as attentive as they could be to quality and says, 'Our desire is to see, in Scotland, a new recognition of our indigenous music and to eliminate, as much as possible, the confusion that exists as to what is authentic traditional music and what is "kitsch". To achieve this it is, we believe, essential to ensure the highest quality of television and radio programmes.'

There are now several recording companies based in Scotland, who either wholly, or at least substantially, record traditional music. Their survival, albeit often precarious, is one of the most encouraging signs that the public's interest in their own traditions has been consolidated.

Not only consolidation has occurred, but also respectability. Use of the latter word has become almost pejorative – it can connote stuffiness, dullness and stagnation, but this need not be the case. Respectability is just what the folk movement has needed in many ways, as the conventional sixties and seventies image of the folk-singer, with his wild hair, excessive drinking habits and radical politics, grossly generalized as this was, was not one to encourage the average investor. With respectability comes the encouragement and funding of influential bodies and greater freedom, even at the expense of a little of the Bohemian spirit. Only one example of this change in attitude is the British Council, who at one time were loath to send traditional musicians abroad, fearing the worst about their ambassadorial qualities, and preferred to stick to classical representatives. Now the picture has altered considerably, and traditional musicians are sent as far afield as Africa by the Council, winning considerable good-will from those they entertain. Bridges are being built, moreover, between traditional music and classical; experiments bringing the indigenous instruments into the conventional orchestra setting have proved very successful, not only musically, but as a significant step towards finally dispelling snobbish attitudes on the part of the classical musicians and the attainment of mutual respect.

Money, of course, is not the only necessary factor for survival. Another crucial element, already mentioned, of any movement such as the folk revival is that it continues and develops, as well as preserves. If this is not allowed to happen, the structure will simply crumble. Fortunately, this has not been the case with the traditional music movement. There are, of course, several of the original prime movers still performing and working, and encouraging others to carry on their modus operandi, but others have emerged and continue to emerge, and the sound they produce is innovative, and makes full use of the wide range of sophisticated technology available, often resulting in highly complex, but nonetheless pleasing, structures and often, too, combining the sound of the conventional traditional instruments with that of, say, the lute, the mandolin and the bouzouki. The Boys of the Lough, the Whistle-binkies and Freeland Barbour spring readily to mind as examples. There is also the Gaelic element to be taken into account. Mention has been made of a Gaelic revival, and the beginnings of this. Ailie Munro suggests that it might be more appropriate to think in terms of a much more recent 'real' beginning, since the fifties and sixties was a time when the Gaels were assimilating the rest of the revival. Now, with groups like the Battlefield Band and Runrig, who are enormously popular far beyond the boundaries of their Gaelic songs, probably because they have combined the 'folk' style with 'rock', the Gaelic 'idiom' has been pulled on to the bandwagon, has become 'trendy'. Young Gaels like to be as up to date as their peers further south, and although purists are exasperated by their poor, or even unintelligible usage of the language, there can be little doubt that groups such as these make Gaelic attractive to their young followers. This, together with plans to increase substantially the Gaelic output of both radio and television programmes can only be satisfying for those who have been anxious about the preservation of Gaelic culture.

The movement to restore and consolidate the Gaelic arts has not, however, stopped there. Concern at the apparent obsolescence of the language and associated skills led to the appointment in 1987, by the combined forces of the Highlands and Islands Development Board and the Scottish Arts Council, of a development officer for the Gaelic arts, whose remit was extremely wide. His report at the end of a year highlighted both the strengths and weaknesses of the current state of affairs and proposed a system of collective funding by the various organizations specializing in the different traditional skills, replacing isolated indigence with mutual support. The report also identified areas of special need and presented a package of specific projects also designed to be supportive of each other.

On the musical front, the report concluded that the focus for development should be on an existing project, started on the island of Barra in 1981. The islanders had become increasingly anxious about declining interest in the native arts and, faced with an unsupportive local authority, decided to initiate their own project. Money was raised from the local community to set up a two-week summer school on the island, and tutors were invited from all over Scotland to come and instruct young people, for a nominal fee, in everything from Gaelic song to the tin whistle. This has been an annual event since its inception and continues to gather momentum, with the best of the summer learners, some as young as twelve or thirteen, providing winter tuition. This event was the first of the *Feisean* (pronounced fayshun, meaning entertainment).

In 1987, Ross and Cromarty District Council decided to mount their own *Feis* (faysh) and provided funding for a week-long residential programme for children.

There were two of these projects running, therefore, when the Gaelic arts development officer was writing his report, and the decision to encourage similar undertakings all over the Gaelic-speaking areas has led to *Feisean* being started on Islay (where the emphasis is on mounting concerts for paying audiences), Plockton, Tiree, Golspie, Fort Augustus, North Uist and South Uist, the last of which is taught exclusively in Gaelic. Others are being planned and it is hoped eventually to set up a *Superfeis*, where children would be chosen from the local *Feisean* to go forward to more advanced and intensive training sessions.

Nor has the thrust to promote the Gaelic arts been restricted to Gaelic-speaking areas, or even to Scotland. The clarsach group Sileas have been recorded playing their clarsachs and singing in Gaelic, by the Japanese.

The energy of the Gaelic movement is enormously encouraging and, by and large, mirrors the pattern all over Scotland. Particularly satisfactory, in view of recent happenings in Europe and South Africa, and the forecasts for 1992, are the initiatives to promote the traditional arts abroad. The Scottish Tourist Board, in conjunction with the Traditional Music and Song Association (TMSA), hope to further these moves and are surveying the international tourist potential of six of the Scottish festivals, which form part of a thriving festival industry, but which have not yet tried to appeal to a market far beyond Britain.

The Scottish Music Information Centre in Glasgow, since its expansion in 1985, has already gone some considerable way towards fulfilling these requirements, but they acknowledge the need for more funds in order to achieve all their goals. Its existence assures the Scots that their indigenous culture will not fade into obscurity; its continuation and expansion would be a fitting tribute to the many people who have given their time and energy to the regeneration of traditional Scottish music.

Bibliography

Alburger, M., *Scottish Fiddlers and their Music*, Victor Gollancz, London, 1983

Angus-Butterworth, L. M., *Scottish Folk-song*, Angus-Butterworth, Edinburgh, 1971

Armstrong, R. B., *The Irish and Highland Harps*, Douglas, Edinburgh, 1904

Cannon, R., *The Highland Bagpipe and its Music*, John Donald, Edinburgh, 1988

Collinson, F., *The Bagpipe*, Routledge & Kegan Paul, London, 1975

Collinson, F., *Hebridean Folk-songs*, Clarendon Press, Oxford, 1969

Collinson, F., *The Traditional and National Music of Scotland*, Routledge & Kegan Paul, London, 1966

Cooke, P., *The Fiddle Tradition of the Shetland Isles*, John Donald, Edinburgh, 1988

Elliott, K. and F. Rimmer, *A History of Scottish Music*, BBC Books, London, 1973

Johnson, D., *Music and Society in Lowland Scotland in the 18th Century*, Oxford University Press, Oxford, 1972

Leach, R. and R. Palmer, *Folk-music in School*, Cambridge University Press, Cambridge, 1978

MacNeill, S. and F. Richardson, *Piobaireachd and its Interpretation*, John Donald, Edinburgh, 1987

Munro, A., *The Folk-music Revival in Scotland*, Kahn & Averill, London, 1984

Scholes, P. A., *The Oxford Companion to Music*, Oxford University Press, Oxford, 1970

Thorpe Davie, C., *Scotland's Music*, Blackwood, Edinburgh, 1980

Index

'A Man's a Man for a' that', 19
accordion, 60, 61, 63, 78
Act of Union, 16
'Ae Fond Kiss', 27
Alexander III, 7
Amati family, 50, 60
An Comunn Gaidhealach, 30, 73, 78
Ancient and Modern Scottish Songs and Heroic Ballads, 8
Anderson, Tom, 63, 75
Armstrong, Robert Bruce, 25, 28, 29
Art of Playing the Violin, The, 53
Arthurian ballads, 49
Atholl, Duke of, 56
'Auld Lang Syne', 2, 14, 18
'Auld Man's Mare's Dead, The', 53

bag, 33, 46, 47, 48
Bagpipe, The, 40
Bain, Aly, 77
Bannockburn, Battle of, 34, 37
bards, 12, 13, 19, 26
Battlefield Band, 80
Beethoven, Ludwig van, 18
bellows-blown pipes, 36
'Beloved Gregor', 21–2
'Birks of Abergeldie, The', 14
Birnie, Patie, 53–4
blowpipe, 47
Blythman, Morris, 74
'Bonnie Dundee', 14
Bonnie Prince Charlie, 42
'Bonny Lass o' Bon Accord, The', 59
Borders pipes, 35–6, 37
bothy ballads, 10
bouzouki, 80
Bowie, John, 58
Boys of the Lough, 80
Breac, Iain, 26–7
Bremner, Robert, 53
British Council, 79

Bronson, Bertrand Harris, 6, 9–10
Brown, John, 59
Bruce, Robert the, 34
Burns, Robert, 2, 8, 14, 17–19, 27, 35, 55

'Ca' the Yowes tae the Nowes', 3
Caledonian Pocket Companion, 17, 52–3
Cambrensis, Giraldus, 25
Campbell, John Lorne, 66
Campbell, Lord Archibald, 29
canntaireachd, 41, 42
cauld-wind pipes, 36
ceilidh, 12, 69, 76, 77
ceol beag (small music), 39, 42, 44
ceol mor (big music), 39, 44; *see also* piobaireachd
'Cha till MacCruimean' (No more, MacCrimmon), 39–40
chanter, 33, 41, 45, 47, 48
Child, Francis James, 6, 9, 10
circular breathing, 47
civilian bands, 45
Clarke, Stephen, 18
Clarsach Society, 30, 78
Collection of Original Scotch Tunes (Full of The High-land Humours) for the Violin, A, 14
Collection of Strathspeys or Old Highland Reels, A, 53
College of Piping, 78
Collinson, Francis, 3, 27, 32, 40, 44, 66, 68
Comhaltas Ceoltoiri Eireann, 78
'Comin' Through the Rye', 2
concertina, 62
Cooke, Peter, 75–7
Cooper, Isaac, 58
Corelli, Arcangelo, 51
cornet, 60
Corries, 77
country and western music, 64, 74
'Cradle Song', 59
croud, 49
crunluath, 39
Cu Chulainn, 12
Cumming, Angus, 53, 58

Dall, Rory (Blind Rory), 26–7
dance-band, 57, 59–60, 62
dance-music, 39, 57, 62; *see also* ceol beag
dancing-masters, 51, 52, 58–9
Darien Scheme, 16
Darnley, Lord, 17
Dickson, Barbara, 77

diddling, 77
Disarming Act, 1746, 22, 42, 43
double bass, 60
drone, 2, 33, 38, 45, 46, 47
drums, 60
Duncan, Rev J.B., 10, 65

Edinburgh Assembly, 51–2
Edinburgh Festival Fringe, 69
Edinburgh Folk Festival, 69
Edinburgh Harp Festival, 30
Edinburgh International Festival, 69
Edward II, 34
Egyptian pipes, 32
electronic bagpipe, 48
English and Scottish Popular Ballads, The, 9
English Dancing-Master, The, 14
Eric of Norway, 7

fedyl, 49, 50, 53
feeing-market, 10
Feisean, 81, 82
fencibles, 43
fiddle manuscripts, 52
Fifteen Rebellion, 43
Fionn, 12
Fisher, Archie, 77
Fisher, Cilla, 70, 75
Flodden, Battle of, 34
folk club, 69, 70, 71, 77
folk festivals, 71, 77, 82
Folklore Institute of Scotland, 73
Folk-music in School, 74–5
Folk-music Revival in Scotland, The, 1
Forty-five Rebellion, 39, 42–3, 52
Freeland Barbour, 80

Gaelic, 11, 73–4, 80–2
    music, 12, 13, 19–24, 29, 66, 68–9, 72–3, 75, 80–1
        psalms, 23
Gaelic Arts Development Officer, 81, 82
George IV, 57
Gordon, Duke of, 58
Govan Police Pipe Band, 45
Gow, Nathaniel, 57
Gow, Niel, 55–7, 58, 59
Gow, Niel Jnr, 57
Gow, William, 57
grace notes, 3

'great songs', 13
Greig, Gavin, 6, 10, 65
'Griogal Chridhe', 21–2
gue, 49, 60
guitar, 62

Hadrian's Wall, 33
Hardanger fiddle, 62
Hastie family, 34
Haydn, Franz Joseph, 18, 51
Henderson, Hamish, 68, 71, 74
Henry VIII, 34
heptatonic scale, 3
Herd, David, 8
hexatonic scale, 2–3
Highland hump, 29
Highland Society, The, 43, 44
Highlands and Islands Development Board, 81
Hogg, James, 9
Holst, Gustav, 65
horn, 31
hornpipes, 57
Hume, Alexander, 37

International Folk-music Council, 1
Invereshie, Laird of, 54
Irish and Highland Harps, 25, 28–9
Irish pipes, 36, 37

James I, 34
jazz, 75
Jew's-harp, 77
jig, 44, 57
Johnson, David, 34
Johnson, James, 18
'Jolly Pleugh-boys, The', 10

Kennedy Fraser, Marjory, 24, 29, 30, 66
Kennedy Fraser, Patuffa, 29, 30
Knox, John, 35, 49

labour songs, 19
Laidlaw, Margaret, 9
Lamont Harp, 28–9
Last Leaves of Traditional Ballads and Ballad Airs, 10
Lauder, Harry, 18
Linguistic Survey of Scotland, 73
Littlewood, Joan, 67

'Loch Lomond', 75
Long Harvest, The, 68
Long Tunes, 23
Lowland pipes, 37
lullabies, 21–2
lute, 80

MacArthur, Charles, 41
MacColl, Ewan, 67–8, 71
MacCrimmon, Donald Ban, 39
MacCrimmon, Donald Mor, 39, 40
MacCrimmon family, 38–42, 43–4
MacCrimmon, Patrick Og, 40, 41
Macgregor, Jimmie, 70
MacGregor lullaby, 21–2
Macgregor's Gathering, 79
MacKay, Angus, 44
MacKay, John, 44
Maclean, Calum, 66
MacLeod clan, 26–7, 38, 40
Macleod, Kenneth, 24
MacNeil, Flora, 73
Macpherson, James, 54–5
'Macpherson's Rant', 54
mandolin, 80
march, 44
Margaret, Maid of Norway, 7, 60
Marshall, William, 58
Mary Queen of Scots, 17, 29, 49
Measure of Scots, A, 79
Melrose Abbey, 33, 49
Menuhin, Yehudi, 56
Menzies clan, 37
minstrels, 33, 34, 37
Minstrelsy of the Scottish Border, 8
Montgomery's Highlanders, 43
Morrison, Ruairidh Dall, 26–7
mouth music, 22–3
mouth organ, 77
Muckle (Aald) reels, 61
Munro, Ailie, 1, 74–5, 80
Music and Society in Lowland Scotland in the 18th Century, 34
Music Makers, The, 79
Musick for the Scots Songs in the Tea-Table Miscellany, 16
'Music-learning in Traditional Societies', 75–7
'My Love She's But a Lassie Yet', 3

National Mod, 12, 29, 30, 66, 73
Nebuchadnezzar, 31
Nero, 32–3
'Niel Gow's Lament for the Death of his Second Wife', 57
nine-note scale, 44–5
Northern Meeting, 44
Northumbrian pipes, 36–7
Norwegian Hallings, 61–2

òrain mhór, 13
Ogilvie family, 42
Orpheus Caledonius, 7, 15, 16
Ossianic ballads, 12, 49
Oswald, Jones, 17, 52–3

Parker, Charles, 68
pentatonic scale, 2–3
People's Festivals, 69, 73
Performance of Folk and Other Related Music (PER-
    FORM), 78
Petrie, Robert, 58
piano, 60, 61, 62
pibroch, 39; see also piobaireachd
Pills to Purge Melancholy, 14–15
piobaireachd, 23, 27–8, 39–40, 41–2, 43–4, 45
Piobaireachd Society, 44
pipe-bands, 35, 44–6
piping colleges, 40–2, 43
Pitt, William, 43
Playford, Henry, 52
Playford, John, 14
police bands, 45
pop music, 74, 75
precentor, 23
protest songs, 67
puirt-a-beul, 22–3
Purcell, Henry, 14
Pure Scotch, 60

Queen Mary Harp, 29

radio broadcasts, 60, 66, 68, 73, 77, 78–9, 81
Ramsay, Allan, 15, 16, 53–4
Ray, Archie, 70
Redpath, Jean, 70
reeds, 47
reel, 44, 50, 51, 53, 57, 62
Reid, James, 42
Rizzio, David, 17

Robertson, Jeannie, 70, 71
rock music, 75, 80
Romans, 31, 32–3
'Rory Dall's Port', 27
Rout of Moy, 39
rowing songs, 22
Royal Museum of Scotland, 29
Royal Scottish Pipe Band Association, 78
Runrig, 75, 80
rybid (rebeck), 49

school, music in, 74–7
School of Scottish Studies, 18, 23, 24, 68–9, 73
Scotland Sings, 68
Scotland's Music, 15, 41
Scots Musical Museum, The, 8, 18
Scots Reels or Country Dances, 53
Scots snap, 2, 56
'Scots Wha Hae', 18
Scott, Sir Walter, 8–9
Scott, William, 59
Scottish Arts Council, 74, 75, 77, 79, 81
Scottish Gipsy Festival, 71
Scottish Music Information Centre, 82
Scottish regimental bands, 45
Scottish regiments, raising of the, 43
Scottish Tourist Board, 82
Scottish Travellers' Council, 71
Select Collection of Original Scottish Airs, 18
seven-note scale, 3
Shand, Jimmy, 60
Sharp, Cecil, 65
Shaw, Margaret Fay, 66
Shetland Fiddlers' Society, 63
Shetland Folk Society, 63
Shetland Isles, 60–4
    fiddling, 60–3, 75
Sileas, 82
Singing Island, The, 68
'Singing Kettle, The', 75
Singing the Fishing, 68
'Sir Patrick Spens', 7
siubhal, 39
Skene manuscript, 14
skiffle, 66, 68, 74
Skinner, James Scott, 58–9
small pipes, 36
staff notation, 41, 42, 44, 61, 64, 76
Stewart, Belle, 71

stocks, 46–7
Strathclyde Police Band, 45
strathspey, 44, 52–3, 56, 57, 58
Superfeis, 82
synthesizer, 48

Take The Floor, 60
'Tam o' Shanter', 35
taorluath, 39
Tea-Table Miscellany, The, 15, 16
television broadcast, 78, 81
Theatre Workshop, 67
Thomas the Rhymer, 49
Thomson, Agnes, 50
Thomson, George, 18
Thomson, William, 7, 15, 16
Thorpe, Davie Cedric, 15, 41
Tolmie, Frances, 66
town pipers, 34, 35
Traditional Music and Song Association of Scotland, 77–8, 82
travellers, 70–1
Travelling Folk, 79
Travelling People, The, 68
Trezise, Artie, 75
trowie tunes, 61, 62
trumpet, 31
tuning pipes, 45, 46, 47, 48

d'Urfey, Thomas, 14
urlar, 39

Vaughan Williams, Ralph, 65
Victoria, Queen, 59
viol, 50, 55

waits, 34
waulking songs, 19–21
whaling tunes (Greenland tunes), 61, 62
Whistlebinkies, 80
whistling, 77
Whyte, Betsy, 71
witchery, 50

Yakki tunes, 61, 62
'Yellow on the Broom, The', 71–2

zampogna, 33